INSIDE OUT OF PASSING

By Toshi Yoshida

ADVANCED SPORTS TRAINING
Publisher

Copyright © 2004 by Toshiaki Yoshida
First Edition

All rights reserved. Except for use in a review, the reproduction or utilization of this work in any form or by any electronic, mechanical, or other means, now known or hereafter invented, including xerography, photocopying, and recording, and in any information storage and retrieval system, is forbidden without the written permission of the author and publisher.

All Pictures with ©V-spirit.com: All right reserved and available for use only by permission of V-Spirit.com. All other photos were taken by Toshi Yoshida and Advanced Sports Training.

International Standard Book Number: 1-59196-776-7
Published by Advanced Sports Training, Inc. and Printed by Instantpublisher.com

A special thanks to the following people for their hard efforts to make this book a reality and a great learning tool for the volleyball community.
Erikka Gulbranson, Torie Sumner, Marc Luedke, Tara Cross-Battle, Robyn Romansky, Kevin Hambly, Makato Katsumoto, Monica Paul, USA Volleyball, Tayyiba Haneef, Cynthia Barboza, Nicole Davis, Ogonna Nnamani, Stacy Sykora, Sarah Noriega, Sara Drury, Sarah Urbnek, and the Olympic Training Center in Colorado Springs.

<u>**COVER PHOTO:**</u> The cover photos were provided by V-spirt.com.

DEDICATION

To my wife, Shoko Taka Yoshida
Without her patience, I would not be coaching volleyball now.

ACKNOWLEDGEMENTS

Having the right people around you is one of the keys to success. I am very lucky in that without the help of many people, this book would have not been published.

- Pictures are very important to coaching and I would like to take this opportunity to thank V-spirit.com for allowing us to use pictures that offer useful perceptual information. The pictures of international players make this book unique.
- I would like to thank all of the players for their patience in performing the necessary demonstrations in order to gather pictures for the book.
- Finally, a special acknowledgement has to go to Monica Paul, Erikka Gulbranson, and Torie Sumner. Honestly speaking, writing a book is not my first priority. I am spending all of my time making the USA team strong for the upcoming 2004 Olympic Games in Athens, Greece. In order to make the USA players better, I have been gathering information on different passing techniques since 2001. Meanwhile, Monica and Erikka told me that USA coaches need additional information in order to make their training and technical instruction better so I convinced myself that I should share this information with other coaches. Obviously, I am so busy with coaching that I felt I could not finish this due to lack of time. However, Monica and Erikka kept encouraging me to finish writing this book and actually helped me in so many ways. Without their encouragement and help, you would never be reading this book.

Thank you.

Toshi Yoshida

CONTENTS

PREFACE……………………………………………………..i

INTRODUCTION………………………………………………1

CHAPTER 1:   EIGHT KEYS TO PASSING……..………….....9

CHAPTER 2:   MENTAL ASPECT OF PASSING……………........43

CHAPTER 3:   MUCH MORE TO IMPROVE………………………..50

CHAPTER 4:   DRILLS……………………………………….........83

CHAPTER 5:   TEAM PASSING………………………..……..140

CHAPTER 6:   PASSING PATTERNS AROUND THE WORLD…..159

CHAPTER 7:   5 MINUTE DRILLS…………………………….......212

APPENDIX……………………………………………….......228

ABOUT THE AUTHOR…………………………....…….......233

ABOUT THE EDITOR……………………………………...........234

Preface

Why only passing?

Why does this book focus only on passing? There are so many other skills we need to discuss and focus on. Volleyball is absolutely one of the most popular women's sports in the USA. Even though volleyball is behind other ball sports such as basketball in terms of the number of players or existing professional leagues, it is still my opinion that volleyball in the United States could be even bigger.

Fortunately, I have had various opportunities to observe players of many different skill levels and ages in many different countries around the world. Honestly speaking from my experience, in comparison to other countries (especially Asian countries like China, Japan and Korea or even Russia and Brazil), I would have to say that the basic ball control levels of USA youth age players is a little bit behind. A little? Okay, if I go a little further, I might have to say that there is a huge gap between USA players and players from foreign countries. This may be due to the lack of training time or insufficient ball control drills being used. We all know that good ball control technique is needed to play quality volleyball.

We have extremely good athletes here in the United States but unfortunately they are very inexperienced in ball control. Many of these athletes that haven't been trained well will finish their playing careers without realizing how good they could have been. More importantly, I am aware that we need better and more consistent passers in the USA because from my experience this is probably the most important factor in competition against the highest international opponent. I assume that we could possibly be losing thousands or possibly millions of players who could potentially be extremely good players at a very high level but it seems that there may be a lack of time by the coaches or a lack of commitment by the players to be trained when the players are young. That is a BAD MISS (you'll understand later ☺). The good news is that we are making strides in developing our youth in a great effort by the men and women working in the USA Volleyball High Performance Developmental Program.

As I said earlier, systems do not necessarily determine success, we must focus on all related skills, but *passing is absolutely one of the most important skills in volleyball.* Passing includes but is not limited to basic ball control skills such as the fundamentals of forearm passing. Because millions of players are struggling to consistently pass a ball well in the United States, I thought that it was worth my time to write a book that focused only on passing. I believe that the general concept of skill acquisition and skill development in passing can be learned through the detail and description in this book.

Passing is one of most sensitive skills among all individual volleyball skills. It is related so much to the players' mentality. Passing performance is affected by a player's emotion because there is time between a referee's whistle. Time creates thought in a player's mind and temporarily distracts players. Passing like serving, which is one of the first plays, is a very unique and important volleyball skill.

The above thoughts "baffled my mind" and forced me to make the decision to finish this book. Although many of you might be interested in an overview of all skills related to volleyball and its systems, my current schedule does not allow me to do so. At this time, passing techniques and systems concurrent with my philosophy are discussed in this book. My thoughts are that this could be very useful information for many coaches if they are modest enough to learn something about coaching and teaching from someone else.

Why so much information?

You have to teach your players something that you can believe in, which may not be an easy thing to do because you often don't know what to believe. Coaching is the process of believing yourself. Once you find something that might work for you and your players, you've got to stick with it for a long time. Otherwise, players will never get enough repetition in order to get the automatic execution of the skills.

Although we are all trying to find one ultimate teaching method to help all players on our team, it is good to have a lot of information and knowledge on teaching in order to understand various ways to execute skills and systems. You may have various physical types in players, such as height, length of limbs, body proportion, muscle strength, and certain mental characteristics like on and off-court behavior but coaches must adapt training to fit each player. Unlike the way everyone wears different sizes in their clothes, coaches must have a uniform way to correct problems.

I think it is true that some players are born with a great feeling of the ball and great eye-hand coordination to control the ball. I also realize that only very skilled volleyball players can reach the Olympic level. However, I believe that there is always room for improvement. I am always trying to find new ways to train my players because as a professional volleyball coach, it is my goal to bring out the best skills in each player.

I will use professional golfers as an example. Golfers spend 365 days a year searching for the perfect swing. Although you have already established solid technique, you might have to deal with a slump and ask yourself, "Why am I struggling with this?" As a coach, I want to give my players an answer or a suggestion that I think they should try. I cannot ignore their painful experience. This was one of my biggest focuses in writing this book.

The information in this book will take you into *the specifics of coaching passing* and will provide you with information that you may immediately apply to your regular passing drills or as *correction (troubleshooting) drills*.

<u>Training on the court</u>
Perfection of passing does not only come from knowledge. **Let's make a good miss!** Don't be afraid of making mistakes. This is my idea for teaching skills and systems. We may need to lose in order to win. Failure is the mother of success. Likewise,

players have to make mistakes to improve their skills. Players must not be afraid to make mistakes, but they must be "good misses." As long as my players are trying to use the right techniques and the ball goes in a playable direction, we are okay. The most important thing to remember is to keep on doing it without hesitation or doubt.

We want to pass well at crucial times. Therefore, we must train players to pass well under pressure. If you train them well, they will not feel any pressure and will deliver the ball to your target with pin-point accuracy when it matters. In order to get to this level, players have to touch the ball a lot and in many different ways. Only training on the court gives players the confidence to pass well in pressure situations.

Preparation is everything. It takes time to gain automatic movements. Be patient and keep working hard because the process gives you results. We have to do what it takes to become good passers and to be a good team. We know if we do not prepare for the match, we might lose. Passing, of course, is the same. If players are trained well, they can pass well. It is as simple as that.

We, as coaches, are always skeptical of any idea other than our own. I have enough confidence, courage, and spirit to share my ideas with other coaches in hopes that they will be able to use my ideas to encourage the development of volleyball.

Enjoy my world and good luck!

Toshi Yoshida
Head Women's Volleyball Coach
USA National Team
October 2, 2004

 INTRODUCTION

There Are Many Ways To Reach The Peak

You can reach your destination by many means. As long as a system is running toward the goal, the system will reach the goal according to the general system theory. Likewise, there are **many ways** to pass the ball. All coaches have different approaches and philosophies to coaching volleyball. You should not think of passing in terms of right or wrong. As long as a particular technique is working for the players, it is good. The question is whether the technique is helping your players pass well. If not, I would take a different teaching approach to fix their individual problems. These are what I call "Correction Drills." I understand that coaches have to be consistent in the techniques they teach because consistency is one of the most important aspects of coaching. However, you also have to be flexible to handle the technical problems of each individual. In order to do this, we have to understand that there are many ways to pass the ball and many different human movements to consider.

Passers from around the world ©V-spirit.com

We Want To Pass Perfect,
But the Process is Everything

ROME WASN'T BUILT IN A DAY....

You will see players who can pass perfect balls with no instruction. Unfortunately, there are not many players like that. To improve the skills of the players who are not "born" passers, coaches have to emphasize the process and break down passing to introduce the skills and specific keys for the players to focus on.

The best players can only pass perfect 60 to 70% of the time. That means 3 or 4 out of every 10 passes will be a miss. The question is whether the 6 perfect passes are produced by the right process and if the 4 misses were good misses (acceptable passing mistakes in a playable direction using the right techniques). That is how I look at their play.

Once a player masters the skill, they can figure out exactly what they did wrong when they miss. Even those few great players need feedback from their coaches. We should be able to see through the skill to discover why the player passed well or missed. If coaches observe only the path of the ball, the important technical information will be missed.

The *process* will show you the answer.

Good Miss vs. Bad Miss

A **"Good miss"** is

Okay as long as…..

    1) You are in control or using the right skills and timing

    2) The ball goes in a playable direction

    3) Someone else can touch the ball in order to set-up an attack

For a general example,

In Diagram 1 below, a player is passing in Position 5 and the ball goes to the right side of the court (1). Even though it is off the net or going outside of the court, this is a *GOOD* mistake. However, if the ball is going outside of the court (2) that would be considered a *BAD* mistake.

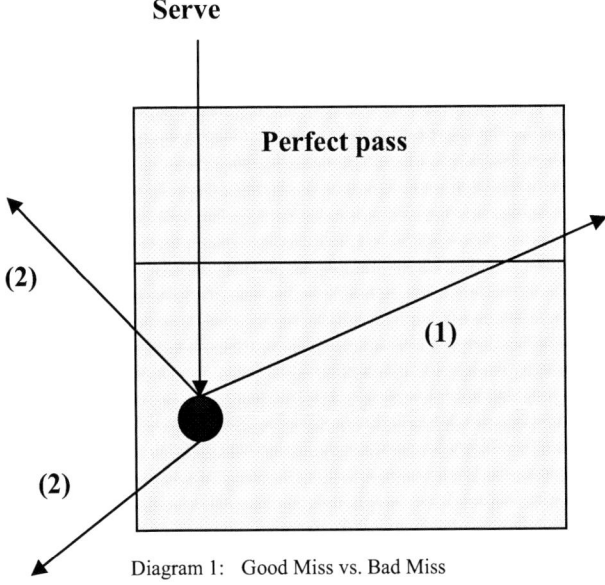

Diagram 1: Good Miss vs. Bad Miss

A **"Bad miss"** is

What we are ultimately trying to avoid.

The two worst types of "Bad Miss" passes during a match…..

1) Ball hits the floor without being touched
2) An overpass

Next worst

3) 90 degree shank: away from the court where no one else can touch it
4) 10 inch passing: the ball is passed 10 inches from the floor and the setter or another player is unable to get under the ball
5) Behind the end line

Introduction **5**

This is How We Practice

There are three ways to apply goal-setting drills to improve skills.

PROCESS ORIENTED DRILLS

With Process Oriented Drills, you do not worry about the results, but instead focus on the process of execution. For example, passing the ball with no arm swing 10 times in a row so the passer can understand how their muscles should feel during the skill with no arm movement is called a forming drill. **Coaches should only watch the players' body movement and ankle angle during passing drills.**

IMPORTANT... *FOCUS ON THEIR MOVEMENT!!!*

This is a very important part of the forming process which many coaches often overlook.

RESULTS ORIENTED DRILLS

These drills should focus on the result of the execution, such as the location and height of the pass. For example, you should use drills like "Three perfect passes in a row" or "No error for 7 passes".

PROCESS + RESULT ORIENTED DRILLS

These drills have both aspects of process and result. For example, "Three perfect passes in a row using cushioning the ball technique" drill (page 128), puts specifics on both the process and the result.

Begin with process oriented drills first and progress to process + result oriented drills. End the progression with result oriented drills with technical advice.

IF THE PROCESS IS WELL EXECUTED, THE RESULTS TAKE CARE OF THEMSELVES.

THE VOLLEYBALL PLAYERS LEARNING CONCEPT

1) **Teach the basics of a skill**

Simple repetitions of single skills reinforce the basics. Learning to breakdown technique into basic passing movement is crucial.

For Example: Down-up technique (see pgs. 85-86) and Cushioning Technique (pg. 128) are basic movements of passing.

> *TEACHING THE BASICS OF A SKILL IS A VERY IMPORTANT PART OF THE FORMING PROCESS AND CANNOT BE OVERLOOKED*

2) **Skills Selection**

Teach players how to use the correct technique in specific situations (situation management) and combine drills with passing skills in a couple of situations.

For Example: Teach when to use down-up, cushioning techniques or both by using fast serve/slow serve drills. The players should learn a combination of skills to promote use of the adequate technique in a specific situation.

> *COMBINE SKILLS TO PRODUCE THE CORRECT TECHNIQUE FOR THE SITUATION*

3) **Adjustments**

Teach players how to correct problems during the match.

For Example: In "5-10 consecutive passes in a row" drills, the player has to pass balls one after another without thinking very much, but with the correct state of mind. The player passes one ball at a time and although the tempo of the drill is relatively fast, the players should be able to correct their mistakes in-between passes.

> *PLAYERS ARE ACTUALLY LEARNING HOW TO CORRECT PROBLEMS DURING THE FIRST 2 STAGES*

Keep It Simple

These are phrases I say aloud during practices and during matches. Coaches should give very few keys to players in order to avoid confusion and contradiction. That can be an art in itself. I encourage you to take an interest in the physiological and psychological factors of training your players, as well as the biomechanical, anatomical, and developmental aspects because all of these factors can help. I am not going to give you any in-depth information regarding the various sciences of sport in this book, but I will provide information about the specifics of passing, different passing styles, and passing drills which should make an *immediate impact* on a player's passing game. The information may also create some *confusion* for you. It is okay for coaches to be confused but not the players. Coaches have to be able to do many things without confusing their players. The deeper you dig to find a solution, the more confusing it is, but this is the way we learn as coaches. Eventually, things

Keba Phipps, USA

become very simple. When I tell my players "TANDEN" OR "TIMING", my players know exactly what I mean.

Toshi Yoshida, USA

Keep it simple!
Give your players a couple of relevant key words and stick to it!

CHAPTER 1

Eight Keys to Passing

1. Readiness
2. Focus on the server and the ball
3. Get the right rhythm and "GO"
4. Move your feet first
5. Incidental angle and reflex angle
6. Contact the ball in front of your TANDEN
7. Touch the ball as low as you can
8. Bring platform back to the initial position

TAYYIBA HANEEF- (USA hitter)

DOB: March 23, 1979

Height: 201cm/ 6'7"

Hometown: Laguna Hills, CA

Career History

Club: Saddleback Valley VBC

College: Long Beach State University

National Team: 2001- Present

Olympics: 2004

Quote: "Toshi's style of passing incorporates the use of your whole body. Passing is not only using your arms or legs. He teaches us to focus on the core of our bodies, or tanden, which allows for better ball control."

10 Inside Out of Passing

Readiness

Ready posture is the position to be in, in order to move anywhere prior to contact. Ready posture is NOT contact posture.

3 Components of Readiness to Pass

Ready Posture- "Stand-By"

Ready Posture with movement- "Sway"

Go Posture – "Go"

Typical series of readiness by Zhou Shuhong, China

READY POSTURE (Stand-By Posture)   Feet Out! About 30 degrees

Front view of Ready (left) and Go (right) posture by Tayyiba Haneef, USA

Chapter 1: Eight Keys To Passing **11**

Side view of Ready (left) and Go (right) position by Tayyiba Haneef, USA

- Get in a posture that will not get you too tired
- Watch the server
- All joints and muscles should be READY to move
- Be able to move at <u>anytime</u> and to <u>any location</u> on the floor

12 Inside Out of Passing

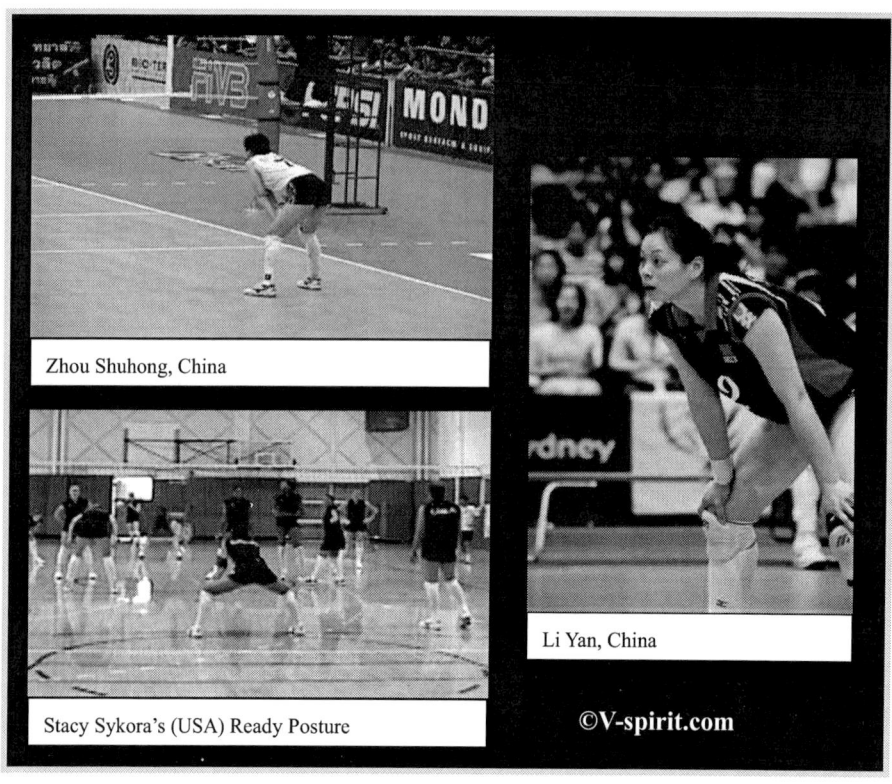

Zhou Shuhong, China

Li Yan, China

Stacy Sykora's (USA) Ready Posture

©V-spirit.com

READY POSTURE WITH A SWAY

Your initial posture should allow you to move. It is too difficult to move your body from a completely static position because you have no momentum. You should have a **cue movement**, which can be compact or big.

Cue movements produce relaxation and a nice flow to the "GO" position. Russian passers often use a side-to-side sway as their cue movement. It is easier to move from a dynamic ready position than one that is static. This type of cue movement is working well for the Russian team.

Chapter 1: Eight Keys To Passing **13**

Natalia Morozova of Russia (left) & Erika Coimbra of Brazil (right) use side-to-side sway.

©V-spirit.com

Stacy Sykora (USA) uses a side-to-side sway for her cue movement.

Tayyiba Haneef (USA) demonstrates a side-to-side sway in "GO" position.

IMPORTANT !!!!

GO POSTURE

This is the most important phase of passing. In this phase, the passer gears up to respond quickly to the serve. The passer's elbows should be "stored" and then taken back when the passer starts to lean forward. If the passers' elbows are extended, it is difficult to move side to side or forward and back to a ball, and therefore, hard to control the ball. The passer should put their platform to the ball just before passing the ball.

HEALS UP, LEANING FORWARD, ELBOWS BACK

Zhou Shuhong, China

Tara Cross-Battle, USA

The ball is in flight and Stacy Sykora (USA) is preparing to move and pass the ball with her elbows back and heels up.

Focus on the Server and the Ball

FOCUS ON THE SERVER

Watch the server. Watch the server's face. Watch the server's body to see where he or she is facing and to get the right information about what type of serve they will use as well as what direction the serve will go.

THE ABILITY TO SEE THINGS CLEARLY

FOCUS ON THE BALL

Watch the ball! Watch the middle or the bottom of the ball to keep your chin down as you pass.

FOCUS → and the body responds NATURALLY & CORRECTLY

After contact, the passer must keep their focus and track the ball with their chin down.

2 Reasons for Tracking the Ball

1. MAINTAIN YOUR CONTACT FORM- the chin is down and the eyes are looking up to follow the ball. It is important to maintain a good platform angle and to hold your contact form after the ball is gone in order to ensure the ball is directed to the target.
2. KNOW YOUR RESULTS- Tracking allows the passer to feel their body (contact form) and to see the results. Results will tell you what to do to create a better pass the next time.

16 Inside Out of Passing

FOCUS ON THE SERVER

Tara Cross-Battle of the USA focuses on the server

Nancy Carrilo

(Cuba)

Best Server 2002

Type of Serve:

Jump Top Spin

Luciana Nascimento, Brazil

Jung Dae Young, Korea

Erika Coimbra, Brazil

Zhang Jing, China

Miyuki Takahashi

(Japan)

Best Server 2001

Type of Serve:

Jump Top Spin

©V-spirit.com

Chapter 1: Eight Keys To Passing **17**

FOCUS ON THE BALL

Tara Cross-Battle of the USA remains FOCUSED on the ball **AFTER** she passes.

Get the Right Rhythm

If you have good passing form but no rhythm, you will not pass well. Rhythm is the timing you use to move and put your platform to the ball. This timing comes from within.

TIMING IS EVERYTHING!

1-2-3 is the basic timing to pass. All players should talk to themselves using 1-2-3 when they pass the ball.

WAIT......

"**ONE**" is as the server contacts the ball. The state of readiness should be either ready posture or sway posture.

WAAAAIT......

"**TWO**" is when the passer "locks on" and moves to the ball. The passer should end up under the landing position of the ball. The state of readiness should be between "Go" posture and contact posture.

CONTACT

"THREE" is as the passer contacts the ball. The state of readiness is contact posture.

If the serve is very fast, two and three are at the same time and the timing becomes *(One) Two-Three*.   If the serve is slow, two lasts longer and the timing becomes *One-Twooo-Three* or *Wait-Waaaait-Contact*.   When the passer has to move to get under the ball. I would say……..

"Move-Move-Contact"

No matter what the velocity of the serve, the passers must wait for the ball to come to them with "TWO" timing.   This is the most important **KEY** to get the right timing.

Move Your Feet First

MOVE YOUR FEET FIRST AND YOUR ARMS SECOND

Keep These In Mind:
- Energy comes from the ground
- Pass the ball with your whole body

One of the most common causes of bad passing is tracking the oncoming ball with your arms. For example, if the ball travels to the passer's left side, the passer puts their arms out to the left-hand side and moves with that posture. I see many young players that are doing this. This is wrong.

Watch baseball and softball players! When they catch an outfield fly ball or an infield ground ball, they run and stop under the ball and then put out their glove just before catching the ball. That is the way to pass the volleyball. Move your feet first and put your arms out just before passing. * Photos compliments of the Vanguard University Athletic Department

Chapter 1: Eight Keys To Passing **21**

This is a catching drill and an over exaggeration demo for moving your feet first and getting ready to touch the ball with your arms second. Players should bring the ball to Tanden and then toss the ball back with the correct passing posture.

Move with "GO" position and catch the ball

Tara Cross-Battle, USA

22 Inside Out of Passing

Move with "GO" position and pass the ball

Sarah Drury of the USA is moving with Go position (1, 2 and 3) to her left side, then puts her arms down in front of her Tanden to contact the ball.

Chapter 1: Eight Keys To Passing **23**

FOOTWORK

Shuffle footwork is the most basic fundamental movement in all sports. For volleyball, shuffle steps are very important in all skills. Players might have to use cross-over steps if the ball travels 10-12 feet away from them. Otherwise, players should use shuffle footwork to move their feet every time. Why? Because you can keep your shoulders square to the target and it is much easier to move in another direction if you have to.

One-step distance: one shuffle

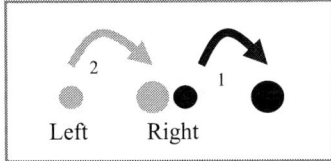

Two-step distance: two shuffle

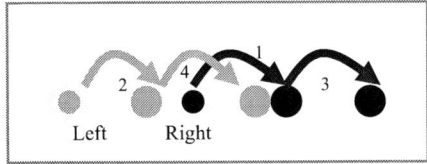

Three-step distance: jab step and cross over

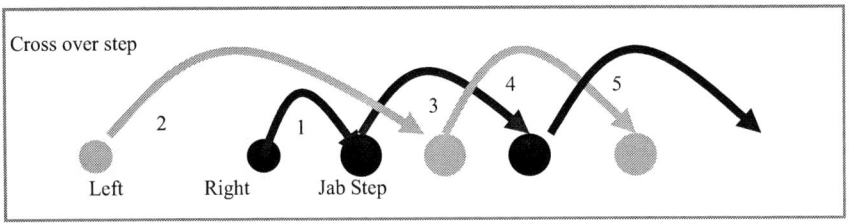

24 Inside Out of Passing

Shuffle Step

This is fundamental footwork that needs to be learned first.

Cynthia Barboza, USA

Cross Over Step

This footwork is appropriate to cover more of the court.

Tara Cross-Battle, USA

Chapter 1: Eight Keys To Passing 25

FOOTWORK EXERCISE #1: Single push-off SQUARE DRILL

Stacy Sykora (USA) moves to her right diagonal forward, left diagonal forward, right diagonal backward and left diagonal backward. Do these 2 to 3 sets very fast. The key is *a big push off.* Her push off action is strong and excellent as she moves her feet first and puts her arms together second.

#1 Right Diagonal Forward

#2 Left Diagonal Forward

26 Inside Out of Passing

#3 & #4 Left & Right Diagonal Backward

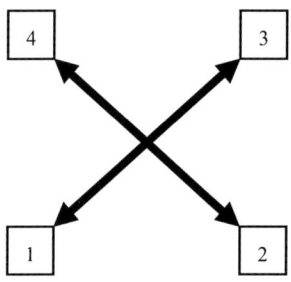

FOOTWORK EXERCISE #2: SQUARE DRILL with Double push off
We can use *double push off action* to execute the square drill.

Push Off to start forward momentum (left) & Push Off to attack dig (right).

Chapter 1: Eight Keys To Passing **27**

FOOTWORK EXERCISE #3: SQUARE DRILL with over exaggerations and both elbows down technique. This exercise is good for flexibility technique training and can be used to enforce passing/digging movement. Although Stacy is very athletic, this drill can be used for players of any skill level.

28 Inside Out of Passing

Chapter 1: Eight Keys To Passing **29**

FOOTWORK EXERCISE #4: Coach throws the ball to the passer and they move their feet to the place they can let the ball bounce between their legs. This is a very good footwork drill, while players also learn how to move behind the ball.

Nicole Davis, USA

Between legs 2 (move backward) This is a very important drill for teaching backward movement to pass the ball. Start with 1-3 steps backward and then progress to 3-4 steps backward with shuffle back footwork.

Nicole Davis, USA

ENERGY COMES FROM THE GROUND

Energy moves from the bottom to the top (from feet to hands) which is a principle for all skills.

Force Production & Force Reduction

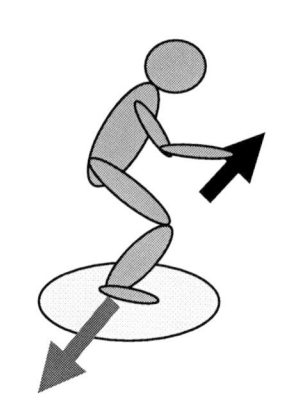

Force Production is to be against *GRAVITY*. When you produce force, you will receive force of repulsion from the ground. You must push off of the floor to move. *Muscle strength is to create Force Production and support Force Reduction.*

Force Production   **Force Reduction** (adjust to gravity)

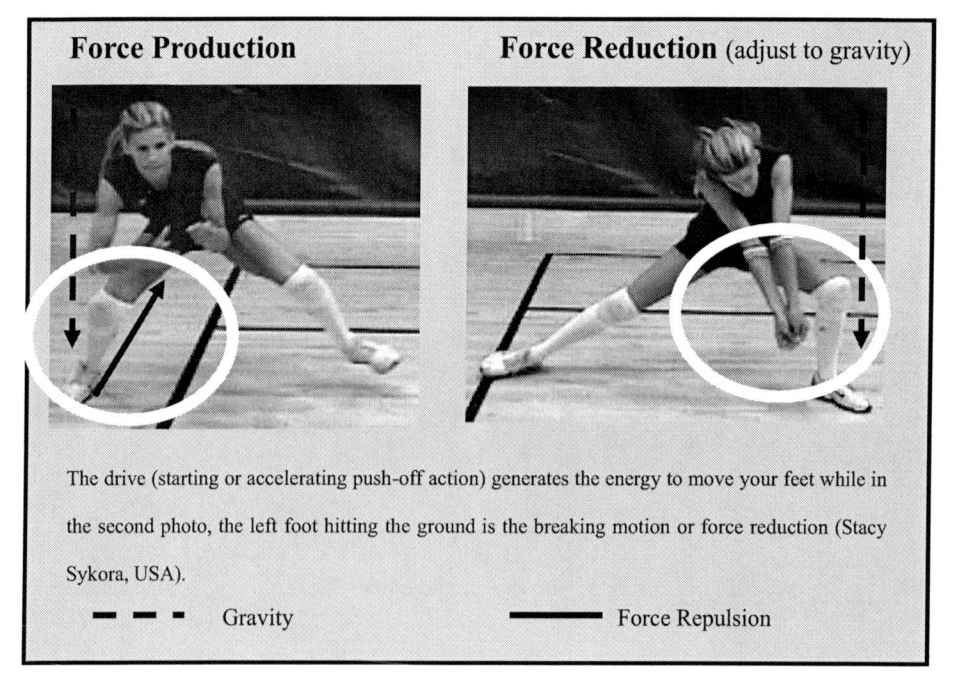

The drive (starting or accelerating push-off action) generates the energy to move your feet while in the second photo, the left foot hitting the ground is the breaking motion or force reduction (Stacy Sykora, USA).

■ ■ ■   Gravity   ──── Force Repulsion

There is another way to initiate movement which includes only using force reduction. However, it will not be discussed in this book.

Chapter 1: Eight Keys To Passing **31**

TWIST MOVEMENT

1. Balanced, defensive position

2. Twist the pelvis and take a jab step simultaneously

3. Knee follows pelvis automatically (Toshi Yoshida, USA)

We know we have to move our feet first. Try rotating your pelvis! Twist your pelvis to the inside and your leg and upper body will follow automatically. This action allows your leg to move much quicker and therefore, allows your feet to move to cover a greater distance. Be aware of the angle of your shoulders. Shoulders must remain in the same angle as long as possible.

Principle of Incidental and Reflection Angle

This is a very important principle of physics that applies to passing.

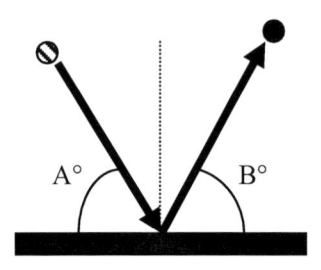

A° is called *incidental angle*. B° is called reflex angle. When the object flies and hits into the wall with A°, the object bounces off the wall with B°. In this case, A° equals B°. So if the A° is 60 degrees, then the B° is also 60 degrees. This is the principle of incidental angle and reflex angle. The wall would be the platform (two forearms) and the object is the ball.

Examples of Incidental and Reflection Angles

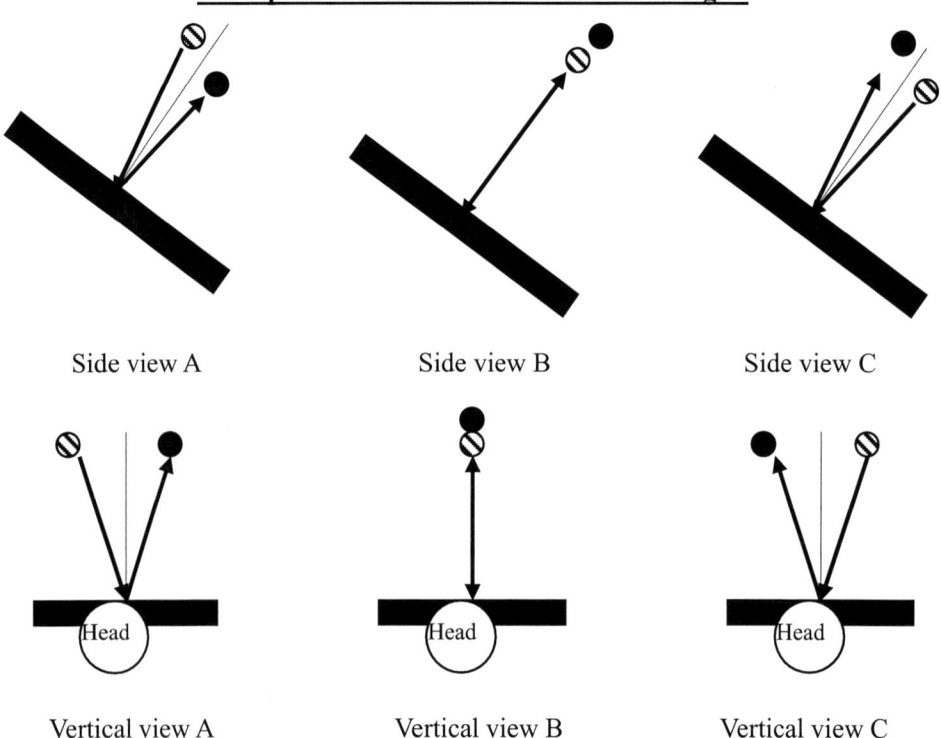

Side view A

Side view B

Side view C

Vertical view A

Vertical view B

Vertical view C

Chapter 1: Eight Keys To Passing **33**

As you see in side view A to C and in vertical view A to C, the reflex angle is automatically determined by the incidental angle. Those are the basic fundamentals of passing. Players need to create the correct platform angle to pass the ball to a certain spot. According to this principle, the player does not even have to move their platform to pass the ball to the target. The player would only need to put the platform in line with the incoming ball. This is one of the reasons that we focus on making the correct platform angle without any arm swing. In order to create the best platform angle, a stabilized foundation with lower body movement (including foot position) is crucial. The passer has to focus on their lower body to help create the correct incidental angle.

- In the side view pictures below, Tara Cross-Battle (USA) puts her arms in front of her body while keeping her underarms tight in order to keep the pencils from falling. She also holds this platform angle but changes the angle of her knees and ankles in order to move her platform angle instead of actually moving her arms. This is a very basic and important way to create the correct platform angle. The passer must understand the importance of using their lower body to change their platform angle instead of only moving their platform.

- Notice the vertical view figures 1 & 2 which show incidental and reflexion angles in regards to foot position. If we disregard arm movement completely and show the ball coming at the passer and the target is on their right side, it should be left foot forward to make the correct platform angle.

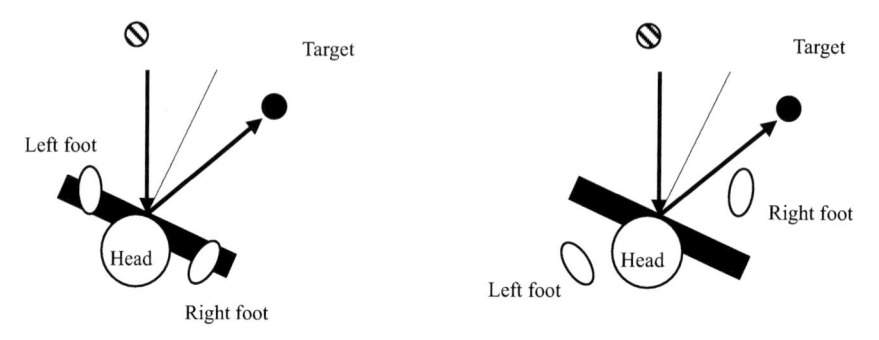

Fig. 1: Left foot forward

Fig. 2: Right foot forward

- On the other hand, right foot forward (Fig. 2) could be used in this case as well. The good thing about the right foot forward method is the ability to shift weight. With the right foot forward, a player can easily shift their weight from their left side to their right side in order to help adjust the angle or move the platform towards the target.
- The left foot forward method focuses on the basic angle principle and arm swing reduction, while the right foot forward method focuses on shifting body weight and arm swing to the target.
- If the serve is easy and slow, there is no problem with either method. However, if it is a very tough serve such as a jump top spin serve or even a jump float serve with lots of velocity, there is the chance of making a bad miss with too much arm swing if the right foot is forward. This is why I teach the left foot forward as a fundamental based on the incidental and reflex angle principal. This helps players to understand the principal of angles and the FACT that big arm swing while passing causes bad mistakes.

Chapter 1: Eight Keys To Passing **35**

Contact the ball in front of Tanden

丹田   **What is Tanden?**   丹田

Tanden is a Japanese word that is similar to the Chinese word referring to an area 3-5 cm below the belly button. It is the center of the body and all energy comes from Tanden. Tanden is actually a spot inside our bodies and is where our energy ('Chi' or 'Ki' in Japanese) begins. The energy is displaced within the Tanden zone. Contacting the ball in the Tanden zone (midline zone) reduces the likelihood of a "bad miss."

You may want to know about **Sunden** as well?
Sunden is in the middle of your forehead. Sunden is also a point of energy origination ('Chi' or 'Ki'). The line connecting the Sunden and the Tanden is the midline. For the most consistent ball control results, players should contact the ball in the Tanden and Sunden zones.

Understanding Tanden

The following is an excerpt from Sensei Joel Chandlers new book, *ISSHINRYU KARATE HISTORY AND KATA*:

The Tanden is a Chinese concept that encompasses the spirit, the will to win, and the drive to win which is a more important asset than power or strength. Even fear or nervousness may be translated as spirit. Fear can work if one knows how to use it to one's advantage. There is nothing wrong in being afraid or nervous; one could label it spirit or guts and get it to work for one. It can pick one up and pump one up. Use it as the greatest ally. The will to win and the excitement of facing an opponent force a subconscious defense mechanism which pumps adrenalin and strength into one's body. One's mental attitude, which starts in the belly, is very important to accomplishing any objective. One by nature has the natural ability to succeed.

Breathing comes from the Tanden because one breathes naturally from the abdomen, pushing the belly out as one breathes in and gently pulling the stomach in as one breathes out. Stomach breathing, as a baby breathes, is the best method. One should not visualize breathing as a nose, mouth, or throat technique but as a lower stomach technique. Think "three parts breathing" - inhale lower stomach, lungs, and then finally chest; then exhale in reverse order.

Chapter 1: Eight Keys To Passing 37

TANDEN PASSING

EXCELLENT!

Sarah Urbnek of the USA is moving forward through the ball.

Virna Dias, Brazil   Hao Yang, China   Suhong Zhou, China

Touch the Ball As Low As You Can

Ai Otomo, Japan   Shinako Tanaka, Japan

** Remember, the lower body helps the upper body to control and make corrections to the platform angle. The best passers wait for the ball, sit under the ball, and pass the ball as low to the floor as they can. The velocity of the serve decreases as it gets closer to the floor, which makes it much easier to control a ball with less velocity than one with more velocity at a higher contact point.

KNEE DROP TECHNIQUE
There are two reasons to use this technique.
1. To contact the ball as low as you can in order to contact the ball when it has less velocity.
2. When you are forced to use this technique to handle a short, sink, drop, or high velocity serve.

If the ball drops far away from the passer, the passer may have to roll or dive to get to the ball. This may cause the passer to lose balance and may negatively affect the passer's ball control. If the passer can keep an ideal contact posture as long as possible, the passer will be able to control the ball. That is why good passers move their feet to the ball and maintain their ideal contact posture. The **KEY** is knowing how to maintain a good posture that can produce the best ball control.

Ogonna Nnamani of the USA demonstrates the "Both Knee Drop Passing Drill" which helps Ogonna get used to touching the ball as low as she can to the floor.

PASS THE BALL WITH YOUR WHOLE BODY EFFICIENTLY

You need a good platform with both arms touching the ball when you pass. So the angle and shape of your platform is important. This comes from good upper body control of the shoulders, arms, and hands. At the same time, we cannot forget core movement (position of the pelvis, shoulders, knees, and ankles). You have to **use your entire body** to pass the ball efficiently. However, when you observe a good passer, you do not see a lot of movement. It looks easy. It does not seem like the passer is using her whole body. Good passers use every part of the body **efficiently** to **connect each movement**. Efficient passers eliminate big movement with a lot of extra, unnecessary motion. When you observe technique, you must also observe what is happening **within the body and the mind**, not only the movement of the arms! Passing is not only a skill for the arms to implement but a skill the entire body and entire mind must produce. Even our USA team runs drills that do not allow the players to use any arm-swing. Make good form with your body, your platform, and create the right timing to use your entire body efficiently. If you find players swinging their arms to pass, use down-up drills (pg. 85), pencil drills (pg. 87), and hard contact or cushioning drills (pg. 90) for a couple of weeks. After that, keep using these drills as reinforcement for five minutes at every practice. Players will eventually understand what it feels like to use their whole body instead of just their arms. Big movements and extra motion will disappear. By this time, the players will be using down-up movement to pass while the over-exaggerated movement used in the drills will become unnoticeable. This is the reason to start with over-exaggeration drills rather than focusing on visible skills. Coaches should always look for the invisible movement, which is often the secret to repeating the right result.

GOOD COACHES CAN SEE THROUGH SKILLS AND SYSTEMS TO FIND OUT HOW THE ATHLETE PRODUCED THE RESULT.

Bring Your Arms Back to the Starting Position

Factor 1: No arm swing!

As you contact the ball do not allow arm swing. Let me explain my definition of arm swing first. Arm swing is when a passer's center of gravity is moving away from the ball and her hands are moving forward leaving a space under her arms. If you use arm swing movement when you pass, you can only control the ball if the serve has no velocity. No arm swing technique is when you keep your upper arms close to your body (no space under your arms) and move your Tanden toward the target. To over emphasize this type of pass, I ask passers to bend their elbows to follow through the ball.

Over exaggerated Arm swing: Bad example by Kristee Porter, USA

Passing is to *receive* the serve. Put your platform below the ball (allow for some adjusting movement) and utilize the incident angle and reflection angle (see pgs. 32-34) to contact the ball and pass to the target.

Factor 2: Attack the ball! Punch it! Contact the ball hard!

Even when you are passing to receive, you have to contact the ball hard. Otherwise, the ball cuts into you platform and you don't have control. Do not let the served ball contact you. You contact the ball first with the right timing.

42 Inside Out of Passing

Factor 3: Bring arms back to your starting position

The principal of the pendulum swing is that the pendulum returns to the starting spot. Movement should start and end in the same position for quick reaction to the next play. This is a basic human movement. This way you feel that you are using your platform angle to pass and it always puts you back in a position for the next play.

THE SWING OF THE PENDULUM
GO-PUNCH-GO

A fulcrum

ATTACK IT

Elena Tiourina, Russia

PUNCH IT

Bring arms back to Tanden

CHAPTER 2

Mental Aspect of Passing

1) No Ball Control Without a Good Mental State
2) Emptiness and Acceptance
3) Automatic Movement Comes from Lots of Repetition

©V-spirit.com

STACY SYKORA - (USA libero)

DOB: June 24, 1977

Height: 176cm/ 5'10"

Hometown: Burleson, Texas

Career History:

College: Texas A&M University

Professional Teams: Ravenna, Italy (3 years), Modena, Italy (1 year)

National Team: 1999- Present

Olympics: 2004, 2000

Quotes: "Toshi breaks each skill down to the smallest detail. He is one of the most amazing coaches in the world and I am a complete result of his coaching techniques."

No Ball Control Without A Good Mental State

If you ruin your mental state, you will not be able to control the ball. You have to be in control of your mind the same way you have learned to control your muscles. Your mind talks to your muscles. Muscles cannot move by themselves. In the brain, the right side of the cerebral cortex controls motor skills.

When you pass, you have a lot of time. The server has 8 seconds to serve so this means that the longest you will ever wait to pass is 8 seconds. You can think of many things in 8 seconds. There is a very good chance you will have thoughts of *FEAR* and *ANXIETY* unless you are in a good mental state. If you are fearful or anxious, your body will not respond correctly.

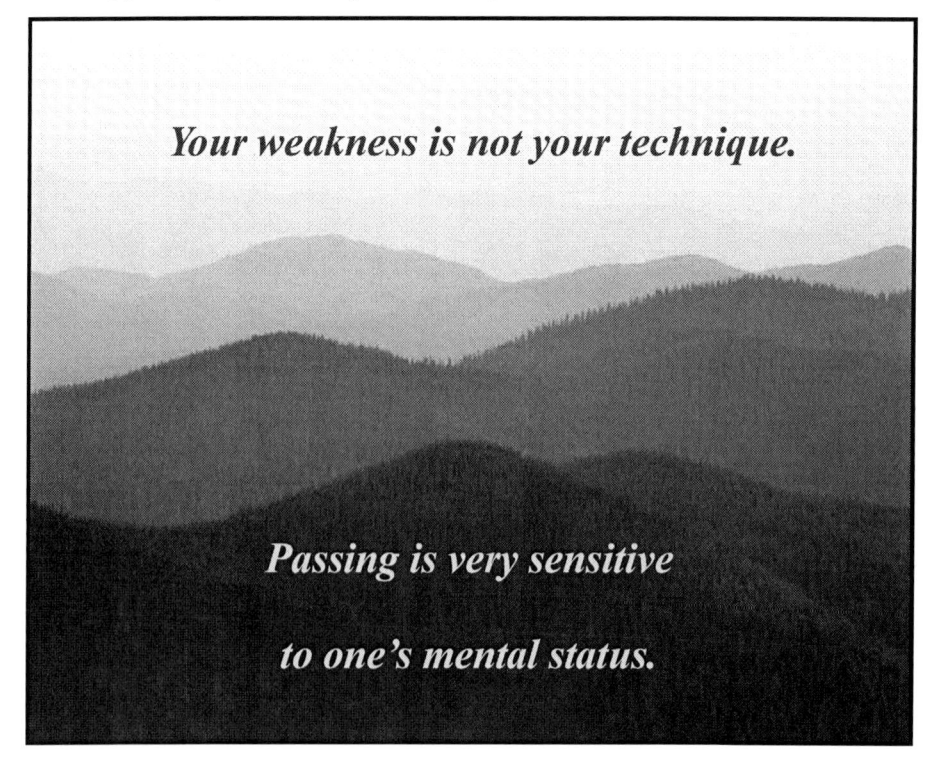

Your weakness is not your technique.

Passing is very sensitive to one's mental status.

Chapter 2: Mental Aspect **45**

Jen Flynn, USA

???? The Questions are ????

How can we consistently be in a good mental state?

What state of mind must we be in to pass well?

Emptiness & Acceptance

The Answer is the state of Emptiness & Acceptance.

If you have too many distracting thoughts on passing and game situations in your mind, your brain does not react well. Sometimes it just freezes. You should not be thinking about anything but important KEYS. Sometimes there may be nothing in the passers mind, but the passer will perform very well. This means the passer is "in the zone."

During practice and matches, when you pass the ball, you say to yourself "down-up," "wait-wait-contact," "bend my ankles" and that is all you need. If you are really in the zone, you are not thinking about the RESULT, but instead the PROCESS and the KEYS.

As coaches or as players, we cannot be 100% perfect and must understand that making one error out of 15 or 20 is still acceptable. Do not ask them to be perfect. However, I ask my players not to get aced twice in a row. Good players do not make two mistakes in a row.
Not two! Not two!

The Question is… "How do you do it?"

You have to accept the results, whether it is a good miss or a bad miss, you will never be ready for the next play and you will get aced if you do not move on from the last play. Even though you hate to lose and you hate to make errors, you've got to accept it, prepare for and react to the next play. If you do lots of reps, which means you make a lot of perfect passes as well as many bad passes, you will be able to obtain a very good idea of what is wrong with your bad passing and how to adjust to the next situation without thinking right after the pass.

Chapter 2: Mental Aspect **47**

NOTE

You Will Only Learn From These 2 Things

FAILURE & SUCCESS

Players should know........

How did we lose that match?
How did I continuously make bad mistakes?
How did I pass well?
How did I become a champion?

You have to understand BOTH.

Danielle Scott, USA　　　Stacy Sykora, Keba Phipps, USA

©V-spirit.com

Automatic Movement Comes From Lots of Repetitions

MOTIVATE YOUR PLAYERS TO DO LOTS OF REPS

Magic Johnson was an above-average 78.5 percent free throw shooter as a freshman at Michigan State and then worked his way up to a 91.1 percent shooter by his 10th season in the pros. When asked how he did it, Magic had a simple response, "150 shots a day".[1]

Professional golfers do repetitions before their start as a warm-up. They do reps before to maintain the rhythm of their swing but they also do correction reps right after 18 holes.

A lot of repetitions give players the confidence to play well at critical times. Coaches and players both know that they have to spend a lot of time on repetition to perfect skills. However, not many coaches know how to spend productive time on this. Typically, good concentration only lasts for about 20 minutes.

GOAL SETTING for Repetition:
Coaches must have specific goals in mind for repetition drills: number of successes, number of errors, number in a row, etc.

KEYS for Repetition:
Coaches must be focused specifically on what they are working on or have KEYS. For example, work on PENCIL DRILLS (pg. 87) to reduce arm swing. Do a lot of reps with 1-2-3 rhythm drills (pgs. 18-19) to get the right timing to pass. Players must know what the coach's philosophy is behind these KEYS to gain confidence in the repetitions they are receiving.

---

[1] Free Throw: Ambery, Dr. Tom, 7 Steps to Success at the Free Throw Line: Harper Collins, 1996.

Without Goal Setting and KEYS, drills would be unproductive and the players would think that the coach is running long drills without a purpose or to take up time. You will see players become distracted and want to stop the drill. THIS IS NOT GOOD! Drills are supposed to be **PRODUCTIVE** and the players must be motivated to do a lot of repetition in order to get better.

The Right Goal Setting and KEYS for Repetition Motivate Players

QUANTITY and QUALITY of drills

=

AUTOMATIC MOVEMENT

CHAPTER 3

Much More to Improve

6 Passing Points

1. Muscle Strength
2. Bend Your Ankle
3. Closing Movement
4. Emergency Technique (including Overhand Passing)
5. Quality of the Ball
6. Keys to Pass-Hit

TARA CROSS-BATTLE

(Outside Hitter)

DOB: September 16, 1968

Height: 180cm/ 5'11"

Hometown: Houston, TX

Club: Ichiban

College: Long Beach State University

Professional Teams: Brummel, Italy (2 years), Nestle, Brazil (3 years), Rexona, Brazil (1 year), Flamengo, Brazil (1 year), Foppapedretti, Italy (1 year), Cerdisa, Italy (1 year)

©V-spirit.com

National Team: 1990- Present

Olympics: 2004, 2000, 1996, 1992

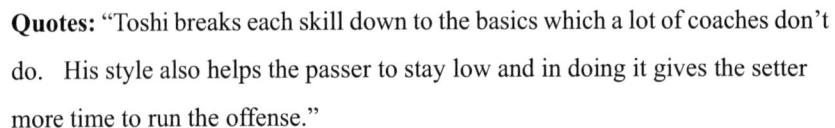

Quotes: "Toshi breaks each skill down to the basics which a lot of coaches don't do. His style also helps the passer to stay low and in doing it gives the setter more time to run the offense."

Muscle Strength

Without sufficient muscle strength, passers are not able to contact the ball in the correct position against a good serve.

In order to pass well, you need *Muscle Strength & Power* to move quicker, to get under the ball with correct posture, to get low, to hold a low position, and to extend joints. *Muscle Endurance* is also needed to cover longer distances and to hold lower positions for an extended period of time. *Flexibility* or the range of motion of joints is needed to get under the ball with good posture and to make the correct angle with your platform. This is especially needed when a serve is coming to a passer's high side or under the knee height. *Balance* (muscular strength and neural control) is needed to contact the ball in the best position on both sides of the body.

Now you understand the importance of the relationship between muscular strength and passing performance. Although muscle strength in the limbs is important, *CORE* strength must be a primary focus of strength training for volleyball players.

"All training is core training. Without a fully functioning core, efficient movement is not possible. The core is involved in all movement and is a major factor in controlled movement." [2]

---

[2] Gambetta, V. & Michael Clark MS, PT, "Building and Rebuilding the Athlete, The Center Seminar: Core Strength & Stability Training: Optimum Sports Training, 1999.

CORE STABILITY

West meets East
Core Stability Promotes Tanden Power

The core is an integrated functional unit consisting of the Lumbar-Pelvic-Hip Complex, Thoracic and Cervical Spine. This is the center of the body. *"The Core is where all movements begin."* (Core Strength & Stability Training by Vern Gambeta and Michael Clark)

The word "Core" can be replaced by the word "Tanden" in the above quotation. Tanden is the center of the body and is where all movements begin. Remember! Energy comes from Tanden (See Key 6 of Chapter 1- Contact the Ball in Front of Tanden on pgs. 35-37). Therefore, if core stability is well developed this helps Tanden transfer energy. As long as you have energy from Tanden, you can play well.

In each picture, the passers' Tanden is being used to pass the ball.
Left: Fabiana Oliveira (Brazil), Center: Olga Tchoukanova (Russia), Right: Zhou Suhong (China).

Chapter 3: Much More To Improve 53

DRAW IN POWER

In the series to the left, the athlete is trying not to let me push her arms down. Although she resisted, it was very easy for me to push her arms down. In the series to the right, I told the athlete to draw her belly button into her back and exhale while holding her arms out. This time it was much more difficult to push her arms down in this position.

Cynthia Barboza, USA

54 Inside Out of Passing

HOCKEY PUCK DRAW IN EXERCISE

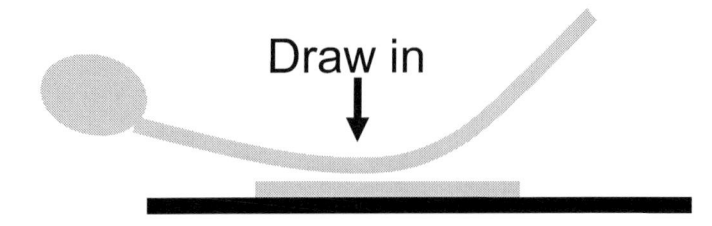

This is one of the core stability exercises that I use with the USA National Team. The Hockey Puck Draw In Exercise helps to build core stability which I believe is the foundation to passing. Players can actually pass the ball using the Draw In technique. There are several kinds of Draw In exercises. In this drill, players have the hockey puck on their stomach in order to focus on the draw in position. Players move their feet in a bicycle rotation, as you can see in the picture below while holding the puck in the draw in position.

Cynthia Barboza, USA

Chapter 3: Much More To Improve 55

LOWER BODY STRENGTH & FLEXIBILITY EXERCISES SPECIFIC TO PASSING

Each of the following drills are strengthening and flexibility drills that I use with the National Team.

Sumo Squat

Cynthia Barboza, USA

Sumo Squat with Both Elbows Down

Tayyiba Haneef, USA

56 Inside Out of Passing

Wide Side Lunge with Elbows Down

Tayyiba Haneef, USA

Feet Out, Up & Down Squat- Heals stay on the ground at all times

Tayyiba Haneef, USA

Chapter 3: Much More To Improve **57**

These are muscle and flexibility exercises for strength training specific to passing and defense.

<u>Front Lunge Step Forward</u>

<u>From "GO" Position to Big Step Forward</u>

Top and Bottom Pictures: Tayyiba Haneef, USA

58 Inside Out of Passing

Front Lunge With a Ball - Watch the Elbow Drop Technique!

Tayyiba Haneef, USA

Chapter 3: Much More To Improve **59**

Three of the Most Important Muscles
Gluteus, Calves and Psoas

Stacy Sykora, USA

Calves work with the Gluteus muscles while the Psoas turns off the Gluteus.

These three muscles are the most important in all physical movement because they are all connected to each other through movement. Coaches should work on strengthening all three of these muscles.

SPECIFIC BALANCE TRAINING FOR PASSING

The development of balance provides a means by which force production can be guided.

ONE LEG PASSING

Work on one leg at a time!
Remember! You have to use the Psoas muscles (Draw in Exercise, pg. 54) to make the gluteus muscles work. Players should feel all of their muscles burning when doing this drill.

FEET OUT BALANCE TRAINING

Get as low as you can and keep your heels on the ground!

Top and Bottom Pictures:

Tayyiba Haneef, USA

Chapter 3: Much More To Improve **61**

Flexibility and Muscle Strength

In many cases, the body is going away from the ball. In the pictures below, you see that the passer is still moving to her left. She is trying not to let the ball get to her left side (which would result in a shank) and to maintain the correct platform reflexion angle. This cannot be done without flexibility and muscle strength.

Impressive movement by CHOI Kwang-Hee, Korea

BEND YOUR ANKLE

YOU'VE GOT TO BEND YOUR ANKLE!

Americans are not used to bending their ankles in everyday movement. Bending the ankle is a KEY to good ball control. If the ankle is extended as you contact, you don't get any energy from the ground. Remember energy comes from the ground. To flex the ankle is to store energy from the ground and to extend the ankle is to produce energy, which is force production.

When players contact the ball without ankle flexion, they have to use their upper body to control the ball. Your athletes might be able to pass the ball if it is an easy serve, but they will make mistakes a majority of the time without ankle flexion.

Chapter 3: Much More To Improve **63**

Russian libero, Elena Tiourina, displays excellent contact form.

In the photo above, the Russian libero's ankles are well bent and the lines from the hips to the head and the ankles to the knees are parallel. This posture is the most stable form to make solid, controlled contact with the ball.

64 Inside Out of Passing

Training For Ankle Power

The drills below are examples of exercises for the ankles specific to passing. Unfortunately, it is not easy to increase range of motion in the ankles. Coaches should work on developing the flexibility and muscle strength of the ankles in their athletes. Below are some specific ankle strengthening and flexibility training drills that we use in the gym.

Walking forward with low position

Forward Hop

Top and Bottom Pictures: Tayyiba Haneef, USA

Chapter 3: Much More To Improve **65**

4 Direction Hop

Tayyiba Haneef, USA

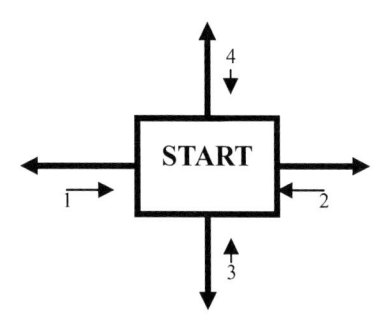

66 Inside Out of Passing

Walking Backward With Low Position

Back Hop

Heel Up Training

Top, Middle, and Bottom Pictures: Tayyiba Haneef, USA

CLOSING MOVEMENT OF THE KNEE

Remember, the lower body creates good upper body posture while it also helps to make a correct platform angle. I must now explain the closing movement of the knees, which is a very important concept we will relate to the stability of the passers' foundation.

Tayyiba Haneef, USA

The ball is coming to her left side. She moves to the left using a push off by her right leg. She contacts the ball in front of her left knee with a wide foundation. The important thing here is that even after contact, her right knee is moving towards her left knee in order to keep her upper body form. In other words, the player's Tanden is moving closer to the contact point.

In the picture, you also see a very good platform after contact. After contact, the player must go back to a wide base position and "GO" position to conclude the final phase of passing. Closing movement of the right knee is also very important in terms of stability and platform angle when finishing the movement.

What if my player has poor leg strength?

This movement is also important to consider with players who have weak or need to develop leg strength. Passing has to be done with a very strong foundation, so muscle strength in the legs and core of the body must be well trained. Hopefully, both legs have fairly even strength in order to have a stable foundation. However, this is sometimes not the case due to an injury. If a player's left leg is weak, we don't see a smooth and natural contact form as seen in the pictures on page 67. If injured, the passer would be forced to use an uncontrolled upper body movement to make up for the weak foundation in order to control the ball. To compensate for the weak side, we can ask our players to keep moving towards the contact point and then through the contact point. This extra movement helps a tremendous amount. If an injured player stops at contact, a huge load will be placed on her legs. A weak leg would not be able to put up with the body weight and good form will disappear. In this instance, the closing movement is very important.

Chapter 3: Much More To Improve **69**

EMERGENCY TECHNIQUE
TANDEN PASSING CONTINUED

SIDE PASS

I teach my players to pass the ball from their Tanden each time they contact the ball. However, if the serve comes high to the side, they may need to use one of our emergency techniques to pass the ball from the side of their body.

Players must anticipate and move quickly to get their Tanden behind the ball. There will be times that the serve might beat their preparation and foot work which forces passers to use an emergency skill. Flexibility of the shoulder to make a good platform and a very good sense of space for the correct timing is required.

©V-spirit.com

Paola Cardullo, Italy

In the picture above, the Italian libero, who is definitely one of the best passers in the world, displays a nice platform and solid contact. Although you don't want your players to be forced to use this kind of technique, this is a movement that your players may need to use.

Another great example of side passing by Erika Coimbra, Brazil (below left) and Tara Cross-Battle, USA (below right) is shown below. Erika is attempting to touch the ball in front of her Tanden even though she is falling down.

JUMP PASS by Chang So-Yun, Korea, (bottom left) Erika Coimbra, Brazil (bottom right). Jump passing is used to maintain a good platform and to pass from the midline of the body.

Chapter 3: Much More To Improve **71**

NET BALL PASS

Passers must maintain their height and center of gravity as the ball touches the net. In this case, the passer lowered her body position, which is even better. Most of the time, players stand up which changes their posture. Players should hold their posture and adjust low to move quickly to the balls change of direction.

Tara Cross-Battle, USA

OVERHAND PASSING

Overhand passing is a good technique for certain situations. Passers must have very good judgment and strong wrists to control the ball.

In my opinion, players must learn the forearm passing technique first. Skills for forearm passing include fundamentals for all forearm play such as digging hard driven balls, free ball passing, and movement to the ball. The majority of serves are not suitable for overhand passing. After knowing all of these facts, overhand passing would be used as a special technique in special situations, such as an extremely easy serve or a float serve at head height.

Tara Cross-Battle, USA

Chapter 3: Much More To Improve **73**

ONE STEP BACK AND SIDE PASS EMERGENCY TECHNIQUE

When the ball floats high or further away than expected, the passer may have to use this emergency technique.

The keys to this technique are to:
1. Take one step back from Go position
2. Make a proper platform angle

Tara Cross-Battle, USA

QUALITY OF THE BALL

Quality of the ball

- Trajectory
- Spin
- Speed

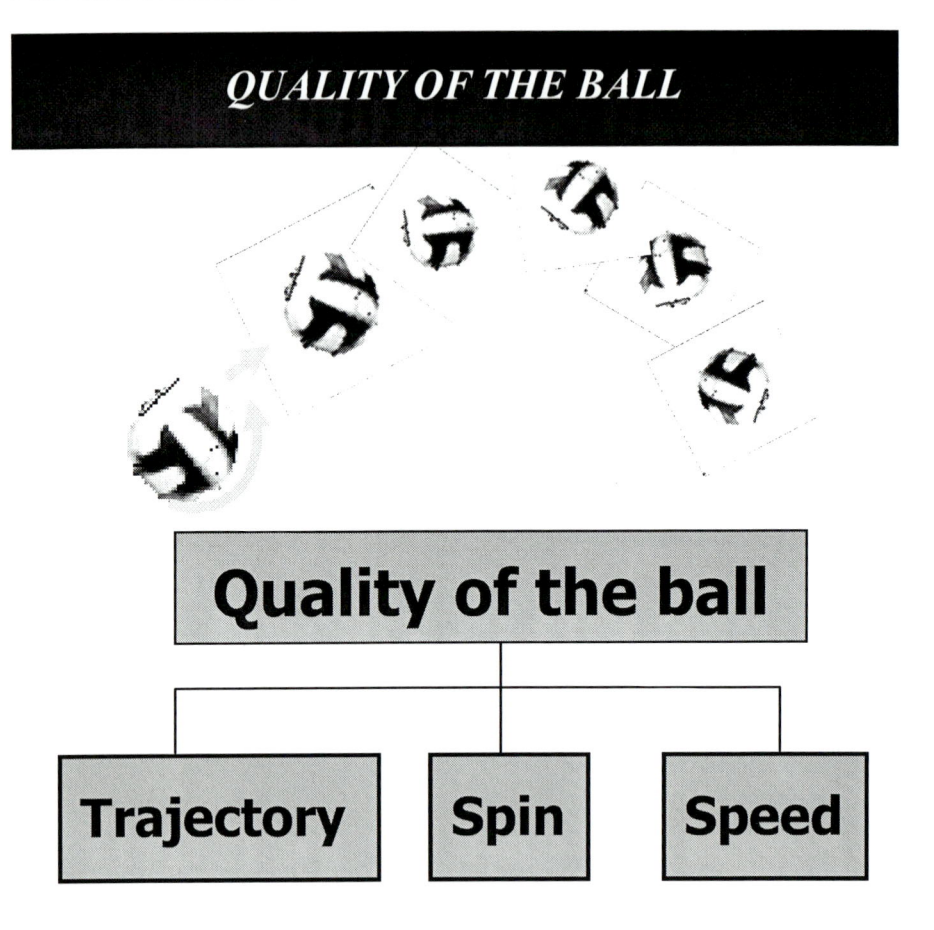

Quality of the ball is determined by how easy it is for the setter to set the ball.

Trajectory of the passed ball
Medium height and trajectory is easiest to set. However, if you want to run a first tempo offense, you may want to pass lower. It is also much easier to pass low than it is to pass high, but it is more difficult for the setter to set low passing, especially when the setter is coming from the back court.

Speed of the Passed Ball

The slower the pass, the easier it is for the setter to touch the ball. Speed of the ball is related to the trajectory. If the trajectory is high, the ball moves very slowly at the top of its trajectory. If the trajectory is flat, the ball still has lots of velocity. It is easier to get under the high ball and difficult for the setter to get under the flat ball. This is why a medium height pass is the optimal trajectory to set.

Spin of the Passed Ball

Back spin is easier to set than top spin. With a good platform and good contact on the ball, the spin of the ball off of the platform should actually become back spin.

KEYS TO PASS-HIT

This is one of the most important skills in volleyball. A basic serving strategy is for the opposition to serve at the pass-hitter to take away from the attack strength of the pass-hitter. Therefore, we have to be good going from pass to attack. This technique is a complex series of skills put together to pass and then hit. The way you connect the movements between passing and hitting is essential. Here are some keys for pass-hitting.

1. Don't be in a hurry! Pass first!
Even though you have to hit after you pass, you need to focus on finishing the pass first.

2. Maintain the form!
Try not to lean back after passing or be forced to get in a lower position than usual before you approach. In order to do this correctly, you must know exactly where the ball is going to land and be under the ball to contact the ball at the right position.

CENTER OF GRAVITY

Evgenia Artamonova, Russia

3. The end phase of passing should be the beginning of the approach.
A pass-hitter must run through a series of movements. Movements in the transfer phase from passing to the approach phase should be very smooth. To produce smooth movements, the pass-hitter's center of gravity should be in the space in front of the Tanden area. In this area, the pass-hitter can step forward much easier and lead into an approach and attack.

Chapter 3: Much More To Improve 77

> Perfect execution by Lioubov Chachikova, Russia, 2000. She passes in all three positions. She was voted the best all-around player.

1: Contact in front of Tanden with low posture.

2: Beautiful cushioning technique.

3: Maintain the form after contact. Transfer phase begins.

4: The end of the passing phase and the beginning of the approach. Middle of the transfer phase.

78 Inside Out of Passing

5-6: Approach phase. Her body did not lean back the entire time and she was well balanced leading into her attack.

Chapter 3: Much More To Improve **79**

The Best Pass-Hitters in the World, 2002

Zhou Shuhong, China, 2002

The serve came deeper than expected, but she still passed the ball in front of her Tanden using the jump pass technique. She then forced her arms to be very compact and quick in her strong approach to hit.

Impressive footwork on her approach to attack!

Yumilka Ruiz, Cuba, 2002

Ruiz was one of the best scoring players at the 2002 World Championships. She passed this ball in front of #17 Marta Sanchez and sets her body up for an approach immediately after passing the ball.

Miyuki Takahashi, Japan, 2002

Takahashi takes the ball in front of the libero who covers behind Takahashi. This is easier for her to execute her approach and she is well balanced as she contacts the ball. Takahashi uses the cushioning technique to take her elbow back which produces a forward arm swing to speed up her approach.

"Bend Your Elbow" Drill is a Good Correction Drill as well as a Good Pass-Hit Technique

The swing of the pendulum always returns to the starting point. The elbows should also return to the initial position because it is a natural movement.

You will get an action for every reaction. Bring your elbows back and they should swing forward. If you do this movement fast, your elbows will bend naturally. That is why we can see the good players bend their elbows to start their approach without being told anything about this concept.

The smaller the arc the faster the arc rotates. If you bend your elbow, the arc swing would be small. Bending your elbows will allow you to transfer quickly from the passing phase to the approach phase, especially when you need to run a fast tempo offense.

After a pass, elbows go back to this position.

©V-spirit.com

Erika Coimbra, Brazil

Natalia Morozova, Russia

GO-PUNCH-GO: A good correction drill for bending elbow repetitions. We also use it to reduce arm-swing on passing.

Nicole Davis, USA

CHAPTER 4

Drills

1. Basic Progression of Passing
2. Troubleshoot Drills

OGONNA NNAMANI

(USA Outside Hitter)

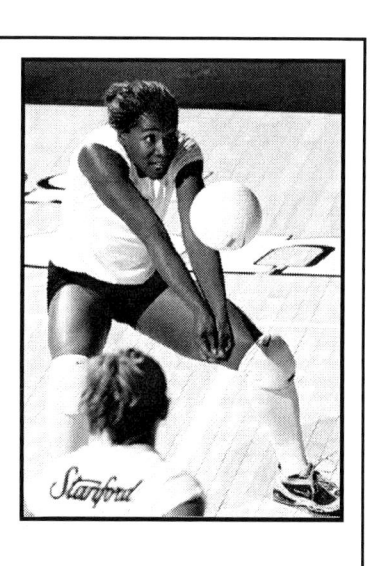

DOB: July 29, 1983

Height: 6'1"

Hometown: Normal, IL

Career History:

Club: Illini Elite Volleyball Club

High School: University High School

College: Stanford University

National Team: 2004

Olympics: 2004

Quotes: "Words cannot accurately express Coach Yoshida's unprecedented ability to transfer his astonishing knowledge, intelligence, tactics and passion of the game to his players. These characteristics allow those that work with him to see rapid improvements in their game that usually take years to reach. When looking at the specific skill of passing what I have learned in this short period of time is the most that I have ever learned. It is amazing to see the improvements that I have made since I have been working with him. It is just a test to how incredible he is at transferring his knowledge." *Photo provided by Stanford University and taken by David Gonzales.*

Basic Progression of Passing

Coaches must learn the basics of human movements and players' skills using a ball, which can be applied directly to volleyball, such as running, walking, jumping throwing and catching.

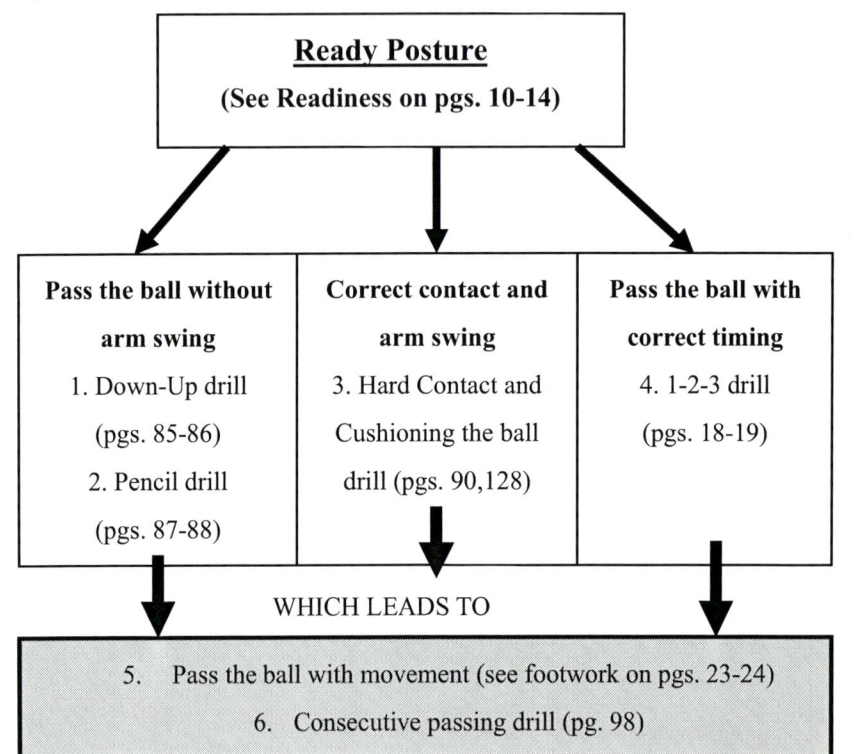

Ready Posture
(See Readiness on pgs. 10-14)

Pass the ball without arm swing	Correct contact and arm swing	Pass the ball with correct timing
1. Down-Up drill (pgs. 85-86)	3. Hard Contact and Cushioning the ball drill (pgs. 90,128)	4. 1-2-3 drill (pgs. 18-19)
2. Pencil drill (pgs. 87-88)		

WHICH LEADS TO

5. Pass the ball with movement (see footwork on pgs. 23-24)
6. Consecutive passing drill (pg. 98)

First, coaches must teach ready posture. Next, players learn how to use their body by passing the ball without any arm-swing and with correct contact and good timing. Each drill should progress from little movement to full movement. And finally with LOTS OF PLAY!

*** Make sure to follow the principle of drill development. Easy serve to tough serve. Short serve to long serve***

DOWN-UP (Technique) DRILL

Execution: From Ready to Go position, bend your ankles and knees to make a full squat posture. Elbows are tight to the side of the body in Go position. Stand or "lift" the ball without any arm-swing.

Purpose of this drill: For the passer to understand that they don't have to swing their arms to pass the ball. This movement also helps to build a strong foundation for lower body muscle strength.

Drill Progression:
1. Down up movement without ball.
2. Coach stands at 4.5 m to 6 m away to toss the ball to the passer.
3. One person drill: Pass to yourself 7-15 times depending upon lower body muscle strength.
4. 1 on 1 drill: Pass to your partner. Move side-to-side, forwards and backwards.
5. Back to #2 drill with movement, side to side, and forward and backwards with a coach serving over the net.

DOWN   **UP**

Wait to contact under the ball, contact, and stand up! No arm swing! Lift the ball to the target!
Tara Cross-Battle, USA

86 Inside Out of Passing

DOWN   UP

Tara Cross-Battle, USA

Stacy Sykora, USA

PENCIL OR TANDEN PASSING BAND™ DRILL

Execution: Put the band, cloth, pencil or soft object under the passer's arm. Pass the ball without dropping the object.

** We use the Tanden Passing Bands™ to exaggerate this idea.

Purpose of this drill: This is an over exaggeration of the Down-up drill. Emphasize "tighten your underarm."

Drill Progression:

1. Do down-up movements without a ball first.
2. Coach stands at 4.5 m to 6 m and tosses or control serves the ball to the players.
3. Circle movement drill with pencils. To learn how to use your body (see pg. 88).

Top and Bottom Pictures: Tara Cross-Battle, USA

88 Inside Out of Passing

CIRCLE PENCIL PASSING

Toshi Yoshida and Tara Cross-Battle, USA

Chapter 4: Drills **89**

KNEE DROP PENCIL PASSING
Use this drill as a lead up drill for Hard Contact & Cushioning drills (pgs.90 & 128).

Cynthia Barboza, USA

HARD CONTACT & CUSHIONING DRILL-Punch Technique

Execution: The passer should start with her body moving forward to the ball (Attack Passing). Upon hard contact, the passer should cushion and then draw the platform back to the starting position.

Purpose of this drill: Players must understand that they must contact the ball hard to control the ball. There should be no time to make a big follow through with the arms. This technique is very good for eliminating inappropriate follow through.

Drill Progression:
1. The player passes the ball to self with hard contact (attack passing) consecutively, from a coaches attack (easy to hard).
2. Move players side to side with drill #1 using the same technique.

Tara Cross-Battle, USA

Chapter 4: Drills **91**

#2 with a Side Step

Top and Bottom Pictures: Tara Cross-Battle, USA

1-2-3 DRILL - *WAIT-WAIT-CONTACT Technique

Execution: Pass the ball with 1-2-3 timing (see Timing on pgs. 18-19). Coaches or players call out "one-two-three" then pass the ball.

Purpose of this drill: To learn to pass with basic 1-2-3 timing.

Drill Progression: Short distance without the net, to long distance over the net. Pass the ball with different distances to work on timing.

#1- In the case in which a player has a tendency to respond too slow,
> Coaches should serve flat with high velocity. "One and Two" are at the same time so you pass the ball with *"Two-Three"* timing.

#2- In the case in which a player has a tendency to respond too soon, (we see this a lot),
> The passer should touch the floor at "two" and pass the ball very close to the floor, while receiving a medium speed serve. Timing in this case would be "Wait-Waaaait-Contact" timing.

CONSECUTIVE PASSES DRILL

Execution: The server moves the passer short and deep or side-to-side for at least 5 times each direction.

Purpose of this drill: To learn how to move consecutively rather than using single movements. Players can learn the movement of passing naturally by consecutive repetition.

Progression: Short to deep and side to side respectively. Then mix all of the directions at least a few times in a row. Serve from one direction to multiple directions.

IMPORTANT!!!!

Pass the ball using the 8 KEYS starting on page 9. For example, when you pass deep court use Hard Contact and the cushioning technique (pgs. 90 & 128). For short serves, instruct passers to use the down-up technique (pgs. 85-86).

NOTE: Before consecutive drills, you may go through single repetition drills with the players.

94 Inside Out of Passing

DEEP-SHORT PASSING

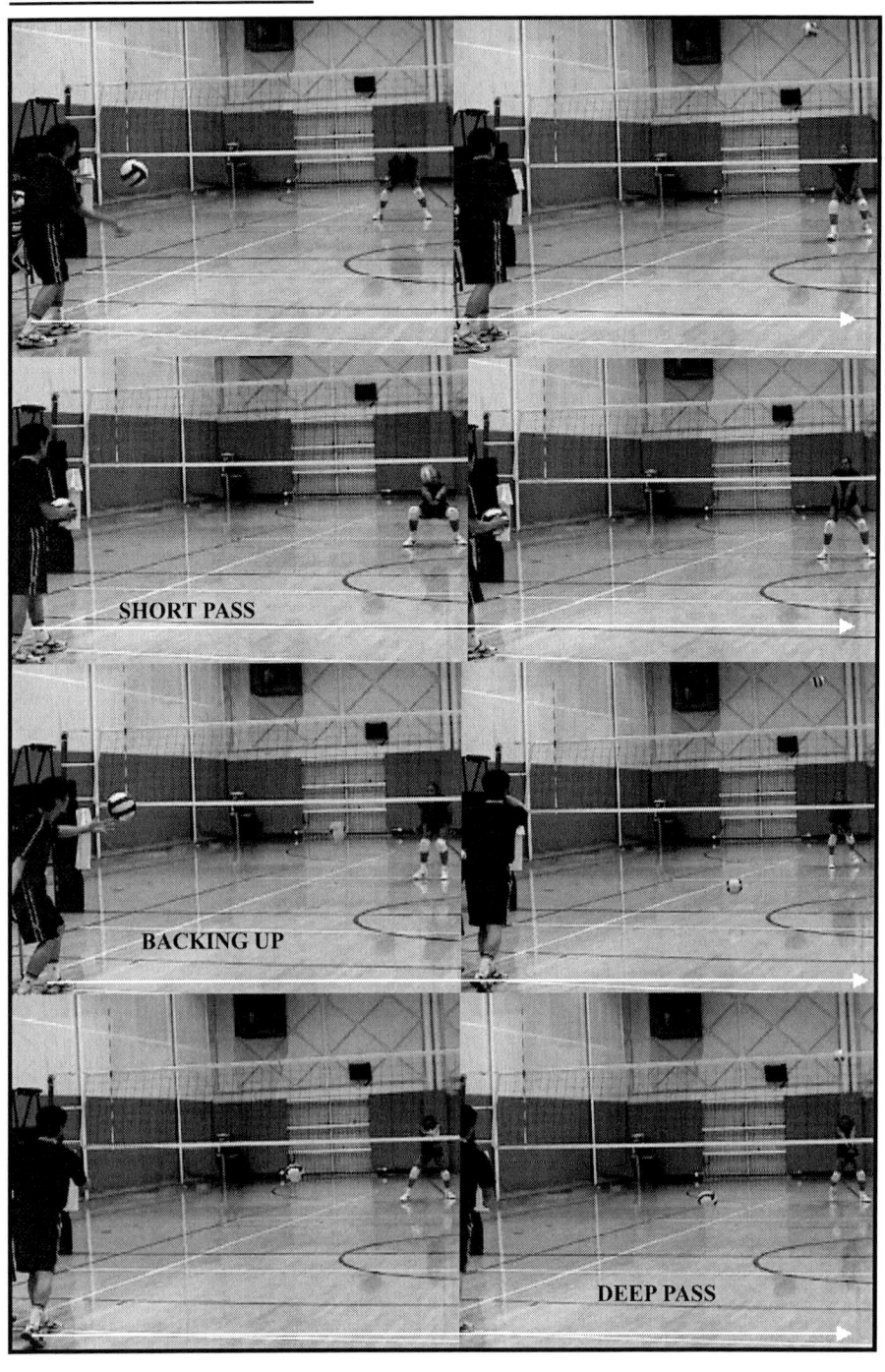

SHORT PASS

BACKING UP

DEEP PASS

Chapter 4: Drills **95**

TROUBLESHOOT DRILLS

3 main undesirable results

1. Shank
2. Overpass
3. Letting the ball drop

In the following pages, I will talk about ways to breakdown skills and correct the problems.

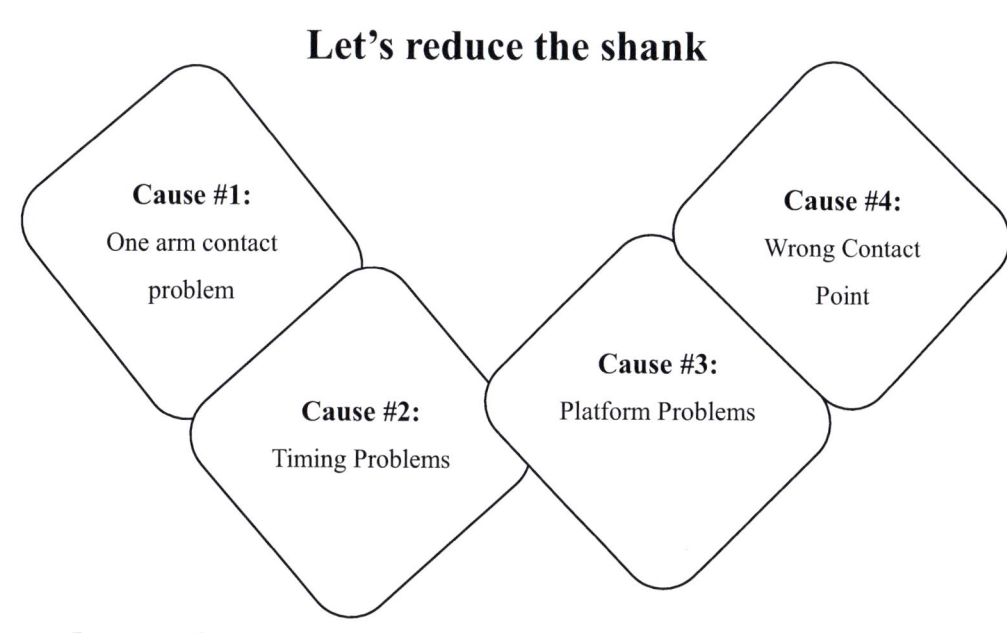

Let's reduce the shank

Cause #1: One arm contact problem

Cause #2: Timing Problems

Cause #3: Platform Problems

Cause #4: Wrong Contact Point

Important! These problems are all related to one another. Coaches must try to see all of the problems instead of just one. Many times one drill will fix the problem but other times, multiple drills must be implemented.

CAUSE #1-ONE ARM CONTACT PROBLEM

This is the typical cause of a shank. The ball must touch two arms at the exact same time. Passers really have to be aware of this and not let the ball contact their arms first. Instead, I ask my passers to contact the ball first. The passer should be ready to contact the ball with both arms before actual contact. This means the passer must take back their platform in order to move it towards the ball. This simple rule can correct many problems. That is why I always tell my players to *"Attack the serve."* The *"Watch the ball as you contact"* drill (pg. 97) is a good drill to help the players be aware of this "Attack-Pass" concept.

When a ball goes to a passer's side high, a shank will most often happen. Passers usually think that this is a platform problem. They are correct! But how could that happen? Because the passer chose not to move their feet first, the ball forced the passer to turn their body and swing their arms in the direction of the ball. The result is the wrong platform and possibly a "Bad Miss" pass. I always go back to lower body work to help with this problem first. Remember, as long as the passer can be under the ball and pass it in front of their Tanden area, they won't make a bad mistake. The ball may still be a little bit off target or a two point pass but this is still acceptable for my system.

Every once in while, coaches may use some emergency passing technique drills to teach players how to use their body to make a good platform angle to the target area. This is okay as long as it is not used too often! Coaches should instead spend more time teaching players basic contact techniques and how to move their feet to get the ball to their Tanden.

Chapter 4: Drills **97**

Watch The Ball!

Kumiko Ogake, Japan    Sarah Noriega, USA

DRILL: Passing the Small Ball

Tara Cross-Battle, USA

Execution: A coach tosses tennis balls to the passer.

Purpose of this drill: To learn eye-hand coordination as well as an "Attack the ball" concept.   If the passer lets the tennis ball hit their arms it may bounce off at a wrong angle.

Progression: Start with no movement and progress to full movement.

CAUSE #2: TIMING PROBLEM

I must continue to remind players and coaches that timing is everything. I recommend that coaches emphasize "timing". This is directly related to visual perception and a passer's personality.

> **HERE ARE SOME THINGS THAT WE NEED TO WORK ON FOR VISUAL PERCEPTION**
> *Vision and Depth perception, pg. 100*
> *Understanding the serve, pg. 101*

Back to Fundamentals
Go to KEY #3. "Get the right rhythm" (pgs. 18-19)
　　1. Consecutive passing drills (see below)
　　2. Quick/Slow Contact Drills (pg. 99)

CONSECUTIVE PASSING DRILL

Execution: A player passes up to 15 balls consecutively with a fast tempo and in a relatively short distance (about 9m apart).

Purpose of this drill: To teach players timing, to make and return to "Go" position and to put your platform to the ball. If the serve is hard, the "go" position is crucial and the player must make a compact punch pass movement with their arms in order to control the serve.

Drill Progression: Increase from 5 reps to 15 reps serving from the ground and then serving from a box.

QUICK/ SLOW CONTACT Drill

Execution: Pass the ball 7-15 serves in a row with fast tempo in a short distance. Use 2 balls and alternate the tempo: One slow ball (free ball), while the 2nd ball is a hard driven flat serve.

Purpose of this drill: To understand when to contact the ball. This drill is similar to the *Hard contact and cushioning the ball drill* on page 90. Passers should draw their platform back to Tanden after contact. This drill could also be used for a *Platform correction drill (pg. 103)* as well.

Drill Progression: Coaches should toss or hit to the passers Tanden zone first and then proceed to the left and right sides of the body. Start with an easy toss and progress to harder hitting.

** You may also add Down-Up movement to the passing technique.

VISION & DEPTH PERCEPTION

In order to not shank the ball, the player must know exactly where the ball is. Near-sightedness and deficient depth perception are two huge obstacles in obtaining the right timing. *Vision is very important!*

****Check your players' vision because some of your players may need to see an expert to correct these problems.*

This is what I do to check a player's depth perception in the gym. I put the ball at a "Real Place" (See Diagram 2). I then show this place to the player and ask them to close their eyes and then move to the ball forward or backward. Next, I tell the player to open their eyes to judge if the ball moved forward or backward.

If you think the ball is here, timing would be perfect.

Real place

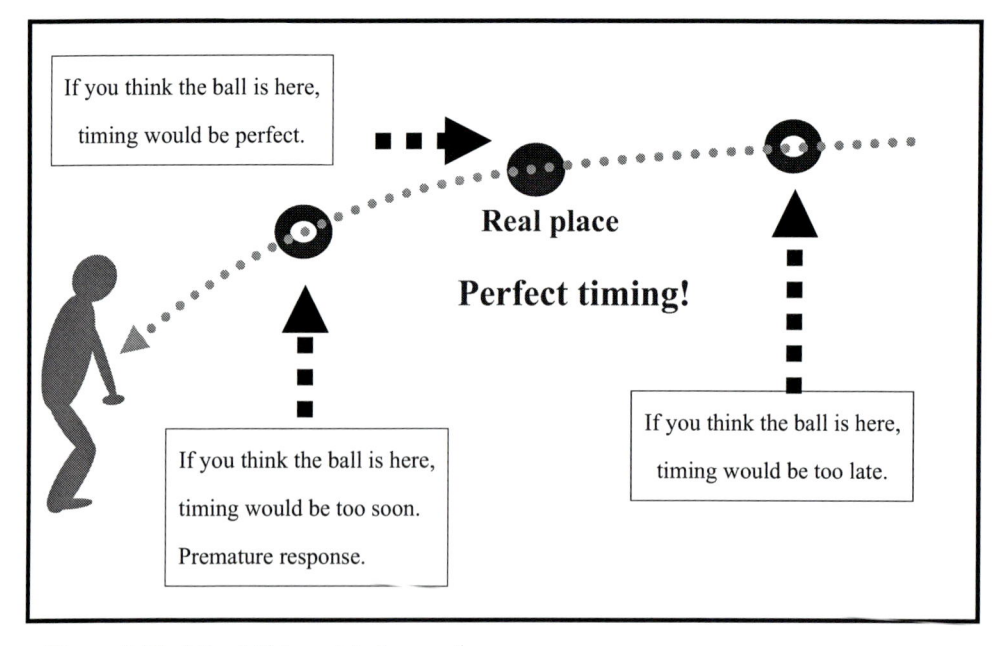

Perfect timing!

If you think the ball is here, timing would be too soon. Premature response.

If you think the ball is here, timing would be too late.

Diagram 2: "Real Place" Vision and depth perception

UNDERSTANDING SERVING IS A HUGE KEY TO SUCCESSFUL PASSING

Watch the server very carefully to obtain information on

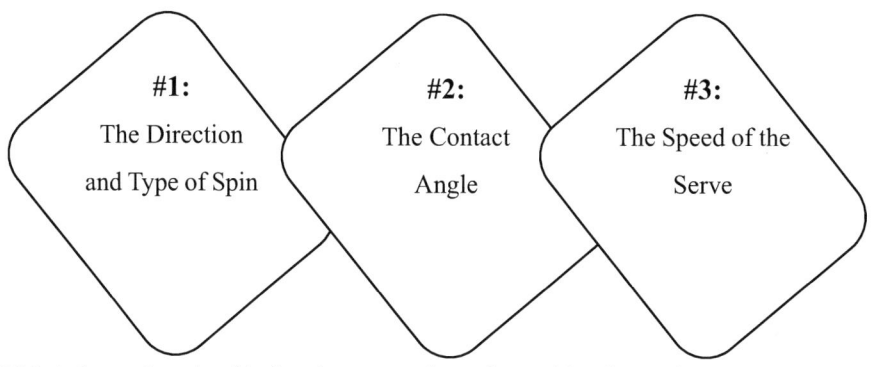

#1: The Direction and Type of Spin

#2: The Contact Angle

#3: The Speed of the Serve

This information should give the passer the estimated landing point.
The minute the serve is hit, the passer should know:

> **What kind of timing you should use**
> **AND**
> **Where the ball will land if you stay focused on the ball**

The passer should continue watching the ball to obtain more information about the ball while it is airborne in order to make final adjustments before platform contact.

Coaches and players should have prior knowledge of many types of serves such as the: Jump top-spin, jump float, Asian sink serve, the regular float serve, as well as the servers tendency of direction from previous experience or a scouting report.

Players and Coaches should know what will happen even before it happens!!!

102 Inside Out of Passing

INFORMATION YOU NEED TO KNOW ABOUT THE SERVE

Type of Serve / Spin

Sink serve

Float serve

Top-spin serve

Side-spin serve

The Direction

The Contact Angle

The Contact Speed

Yumilka Ruiz, Cuba

Virna Dias, Brazil

CAUSE #3: PLATFORM PROBLEM

<u>Platform Technique & Correction Drills</u>
1. One-arm passing drills (pgs. 108-109)
2. Wall drills (pgs. 110-111)
3. Shoulder pass drill (pg. 112)
4. Jump pass drill (pg. 113)
5. Line-Angle passing drill (pgs. 114-115)

Two Different Parts of the Platform

Big Platform

Upper Arm + **Elbow + wrist**

Create a Big Platform & Use It As One Unit

104 Inside Out of Passing

The upper arm platform and the elbow + wrist platform sometimes work separately. This is a good technique as long as the upper arm platform finishes almost parallel to the thigh (see Bend Your Elbow on page 135).

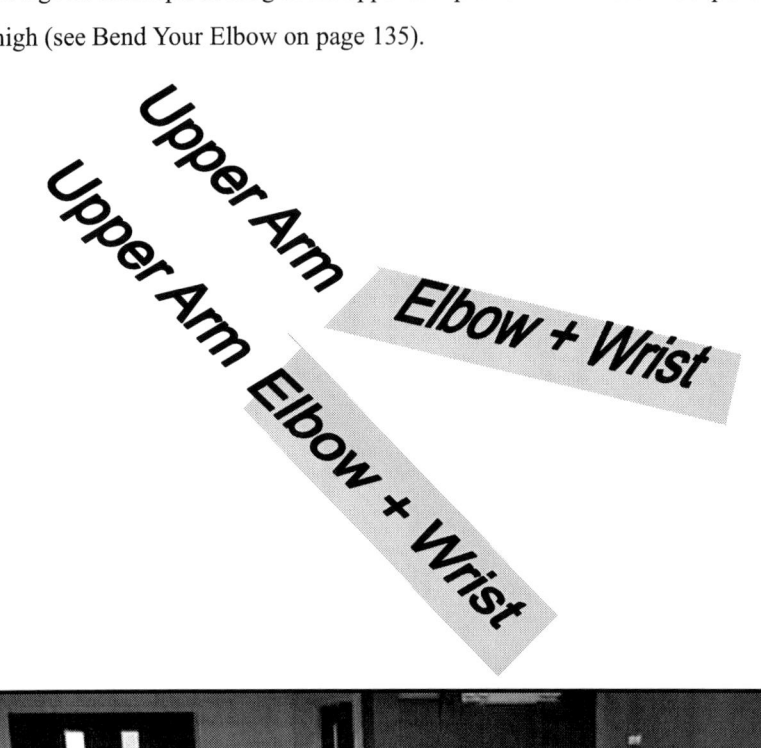

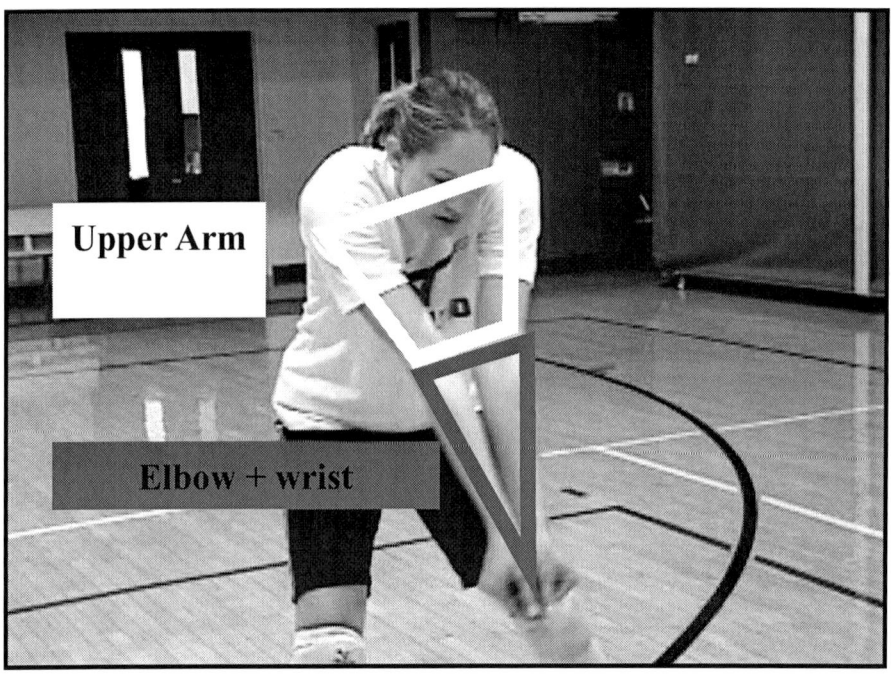

Upper Arm

Elbow + wrist

Sarah Noriega, USA

Chapter 4: Drills **105**

PLATFORM- 2 different ways to make a platform

GOOD

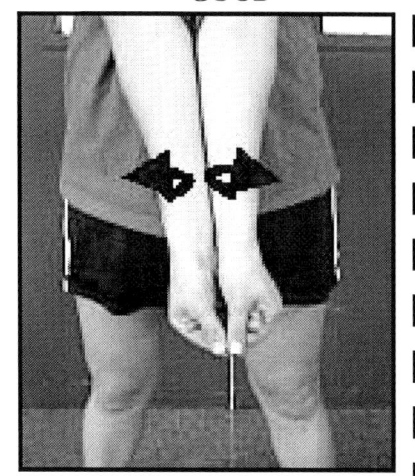

BAD

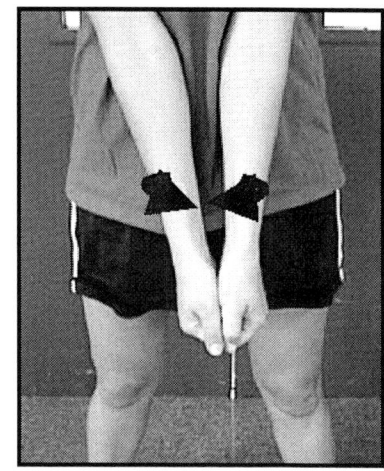

Touch the ball with a larger area and make the platform more like a plate.

This platform is made out of two separate arms. The ball would only touch one arm at a time.

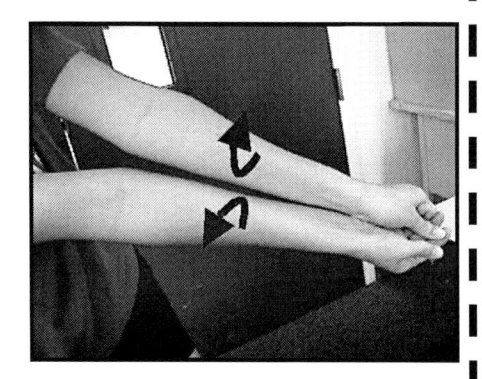

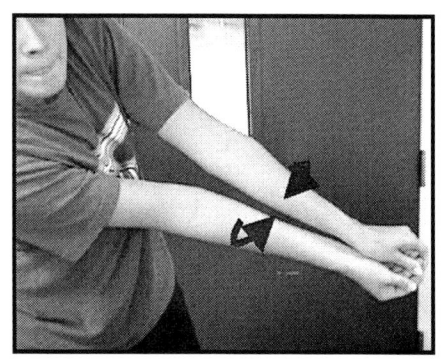

Robyn Romansky

106 Inside Out of Passing

GOOD	BAD
Wrists Down- If wrists are down, elbows automatically lock.	Wrists Up- If wrists are up, elbows do not lock and a good platform cannot be established.
Reduce one arm contact with this technique.	The ball can only touch one arm.

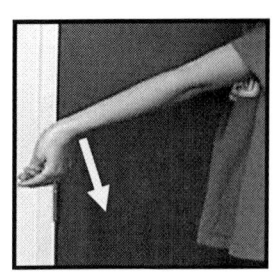

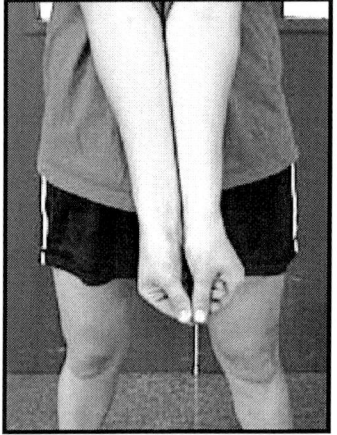

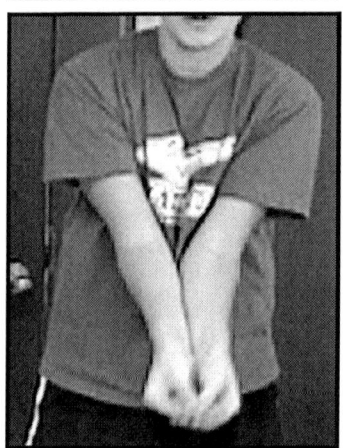

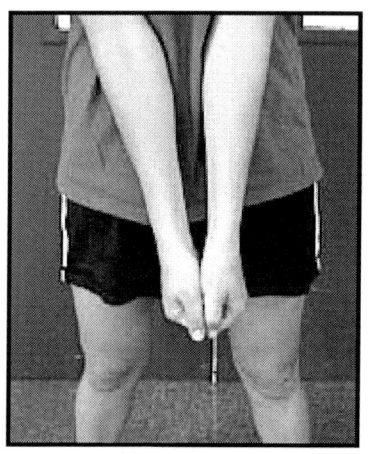

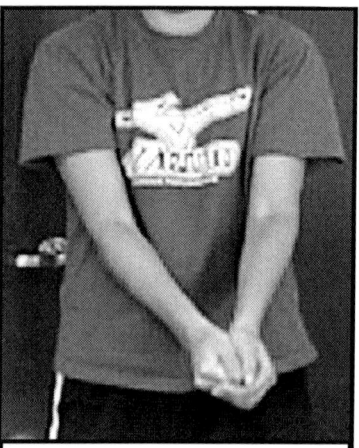

Chapter 4: Drills **107**

| The ball is touching the flat part of the arm and is easier to control. | Only the bone is touching the ball making it very difficult to control. A bad shank will most likely be the result. |

Robyn Romansky

PALM OPEN

Keep the palms open and move your feet around the platform. Feel what muscles in your arms and shoulders you are using.

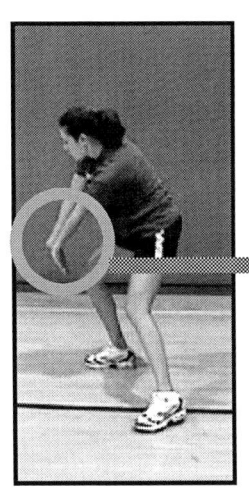

Robyn Romansky

108 Inside Out of Passing

ONE ARM PASS TO YOURSELF DRILL
Make sure to use the flat part of your forearm.

Tara Cross-Battle, USA

Chapter 4: Drills **109**

ONE ARM PASS TO THE COACH (Coach Initiated)

Make sure to use the flat part of your forearm to pass the ball back to the coach.

Tara Cross-Battle, USA

WALL DRILLS

Execution: Face the wall (you can have the player hold a notepad or something flat to make the platform). Move it along the wall up to shoulder height and then rotate to the other side. Make sure the platform is square to the wall the entire time.

Purpose of this drill: To feel core and shoulder muscles during execution.

WALL SERIES #1

Tara Cross-Battle, USA

Chapter 4: Drills **111**

WALL SERIES #2 (Player should rotate a complete 360 degrees).

Tara Cross-Battle, USA

112 Inside Out of Passing

ROTATE THE SHOULDER PASS DRILL (Technique)

Execution: Toss the ball shoulder height of the passer. The passer should rotate her shoulder to touch the ball with the upper arm close to the shoulder. The passer should finish with hips and shoulders around the ball and platform to her Tanden.

Purpose of this drill: This is very good drill to help passers understand how to use the shoulders to keep the platform correct. This technique is supposed to be used when a passer must pass the ball outside of their body.

MOVEMENT CONTACT FINISH FINISH

Tara Cross-Battle, USA

Rotate the shoulder inside first, wrists follow the elbows to keep the platform towards the target.
(Ricarda Lima, Brazil)

Chapter 4: Drills **113**

JUMP PASS DRILL (Advanced Technique)

Execution: Jump sideways and pass the ball while in the air. Maintain the platform angle square to the target.

Purpose of this drill: To learn how to use the shoulders to maintain the platform angle. Many players rotate their body and contact the ball out of their midline. Try this advanced technique to pass in front of Tanden without having to worry about the platform angle.

Tara Cross-Battle, USA

114 Inside Out of Passing

LINE-ANGLE PASSING DRILL

Execution: Two coaches serve balls at the same time to two players on the opposite sides of the court. The coaches serve one ball down the line then the next ball cross-court to the passers.

Purpose of the drill: This drill forces players to make body and platform adjustments to get the ball in front of their Tanden.

Chapter 4: Drills **115**

Cynthia Barboza & Tara Cross-Battle, USA

CAUSE #4: WRONG CONTACT POINT

Correction Drills for Contact Point Precision
1. Tanden catch drills (pgs. 117-118)
2. Knee touch drills (pgs. 119-121)
3. Back-up pass drill (pgs. 122-124)
4. Knee drop drills (pgs. 124-125)
5. Touch the floor drill (pg. 126)

"YOU CANNOT PASS THE BALL, IF YOU CANNOT CATCH THE BALL."

Toshi Yoshida

TANDEN CATCH AND THROW DRILLS

Execution: The passer should catch the ball with their forearms in front of their Tanden. As you catch the ball, your palms should face upwards. Catch the ball and bring it to your Tanden, then release it to the target.

Purpose of this drill: To understand the feeling of passing and releasing the ball from the Tanden area.

Drill Progression:
1. Coach throws the ball to the player and the player catches the ball.
2. Coach throws the ball to the player while moving them side-to-side and back and forth. **The Back-Up Tanden catch drill is good because players learn to step forward after they release the ball which is needed to force their Tanden towards the target.

Tara Cross-Battle, USA

118 Inside Out of Passing

BACK-UP TANDEN CATCH DRILL

Tara Cross-Battle, USA

Chapter 4: Drills **119**

KNEE TOUCH DRILLS

Execution: Toss the ball so the player may touch the ball on the top and inside of the knee. The player should contact the ball with wide feet and between both knees.

Purpose of this drill: To understand how to pass the ball between both knees and to help in the progression of waiting until the ball falls to knee height to pass.

Drill Progression:

1. Coach throws the ball one step away from the passer's left and right knees.
2. Players pass the ball on top of the knee.
3. When players understand passing from the top of their knee, progress to passing off of the inside of the knee.

TOP OF KNEE

Tara Cross-Battle, USA

120 Inside Out of Passing

INSIDE OF THE KNEE: TOES OUT!

Tara Cross-Battle, USA

This is the place the ball should be passed from.

Toshi Yoshida, USA

Tara Cross-Battle, USA

Chapter 4: Drills **121**

KNEE TOUCH AND PASS DRILLS

Cynthia Barboza, USA

Execution: The first time through, this passer steps and passes the ball with the inside of her knee. The second time, I will ask her to pass the ball over her knee.

BEAUTIFUL FORM

The Russian (Olga Tchoukanova) and Korean (Kim, Hee-Kyung) passers in the pictures above both have their feet out and pass the ball in front of their knees.

BACK-UP PASS DRILLS

Execution: Back up using the drop step or shuffle technique to get behind the ball.

Purpose of this drill: To force passers to move their feet and get behind the ball while passing from a correct Tanden position. This is a very good drill to get under the ball when the ball comes at a passer's chest height. Many players will usually give up and use the overhand technique to receive the ball, which would also be a good choice in the beginning. I want my players to try to move their feet and back up to get under the ball to pass. Otherwise, I typically see players with the habit of not moving their feet to get under the ball, but instead swinging their arms. This is definitely not just an over-exaggerated technique but a very good passing technique. Players can use it during the match. Russia, currently one of the top passing teams in the world, uses this style.

Progression: Move passers side-to-side at an angle while backing up (see diagram on page 124).

Chapter 4: Drills **123**

BACK-UP PASSING DRILL (Front View)

** Use the drop step if the ball is coming over your head to get behind and under the ball.

Cynthia Barboza, USA

124 Inside Out of Passing

BACK-UP PASSING OVERLOAD DRILL

Start off in the middle of the court to pass both corners. This is a very good drill, which covers several of the 8 KEYS to passing.

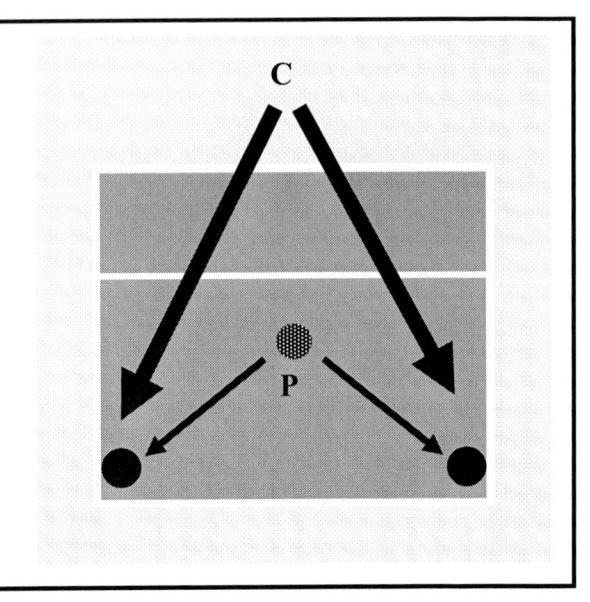

Diagram 3: Back-up Passing

DOUBLE KNEE DROP DRILLS

Execution: Toss the passer a relatively high ball or give them an easy, medium height serve to allow the passer to drop both knees to pass the ball.

Purpose of this drill: This is a correction drill to help passers understand the concept of passing the ball as low to the floor as possible.

Progression: Method 1: Waiting for the ball with both knees down on the floor. Method 2: From standing "go" position to knee drop just before contact.

Chapter 4: Drills **125**

METHOD 1: Waiting on the floor with both knees down

Ogonna Nnamani, USA

METHOD 2:
Start in "Go" posture then drop to knees just before contact

126 Inside Out of Passing

TOUCH THE FLOOR JUST BEFORE THE PASS DRILL

Execution: The coach serves or hits a ball to the passer in "Go" position. The passer must touch the ground as the coach brings their arm back to serve the ball.

Purpose of the Drill: This is a correction drill to get passers in a lower position to contact the ball.

Cynthia Barboza, USA

CAUSE #5 OVERPASSING

Reducing the Overpass
1. Cushioning Technique, pgs. 128-131
2. Absorb Technique, pgs. 132-133
3. Back Roll Technique, pg. 134
4. Bend Elbow Technique, pg. 135
5. Pass-Set Technique/Drill, pgs. 136-137

A passer must kill the speed of the serve and make the right platform angle to produce the correct trajectory for a perfect pass. Using the right technique to kill the speed of the ball is a passers main goal for perfect passing. In the next few pages, you will see techniques and drills to reduce overpasses.

CUSHIONING TECHNIQUE

CUSHIONING THE BALL DRILL

Execution: The passer must cushion or absorb the speed of the ball by bringing their platform back to their Tanden. The passer should focus on catching the ball on their platform.

Purpose of the drill: To teach players timing and to understand how to absorb the speed of the ball and remain in control of the dig.

Drill Progression: Coaches start with a controlled attack that the passer may simulate the "absorb" back to Tanden technique. Coaches then progressively attack harder driven balls and increase their distance from the passer.

Tara Cross-Battle, USA

Chapter 4: Drills **129**

PUNCH PASS TO YOURSELF DRILL

Execution: The passer should toss the ball to self and then punch pass consecutively 10-15 balls.

Purpose of the Drill: To focus on punch pass and to absorb the ball with the legs. You may also talk to the players about body control (lower their body when contacting the ball) and how it affects the control of their pass.

Tara Cross-Battle, USA

130 Inside Out of Passing

BUNT DRILL
The focus is to over-exaggerate cushioning (bring arms back to Tanden) and drop the ball to a target directly in front of the passer.

Toshi Yoshida & Tara Cross-Battle, USA

Chapter 4: Drills **131**

Toshi Yoshida & Tara Cross-Battle, USA

132 Inside Out of Passing

UP-DOWN/ ABSORB TECHNIQUE

Contact the ball with leaning posture while changing the platform angle without any arm action. Bend the knees to get low and force the ball up instead of out and over the net. (Passers should drop their body under the ball while keeping the platform high and not allowing it to swing). Strong muscle strength is required in the lower body. This is a very good correction drill for platform angle work and to increase the players' strength in their foundation (lower body).

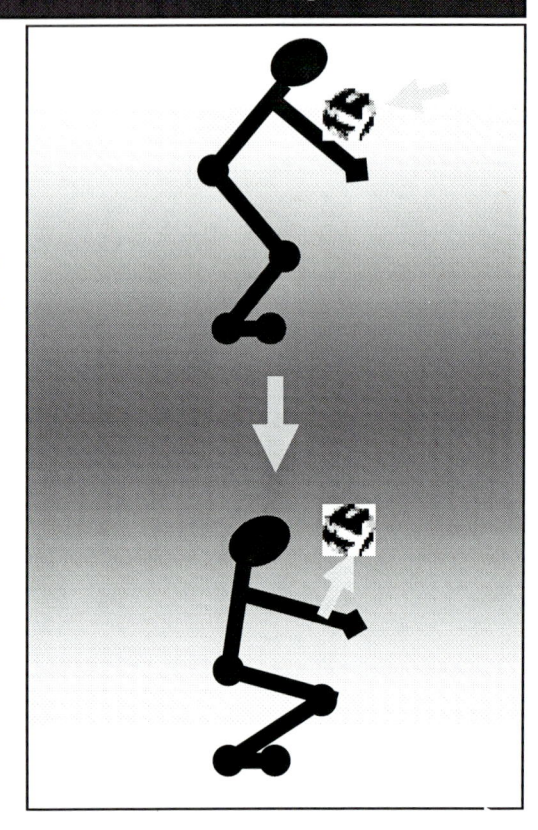

Front view of the Absorb/ Up-Down Technique (Tara Cross-Battle, USA)

Chapter 4: Drills **133**

Side view of the Absorb/ Up-Down Technique (Stacy Sykora, USA)

134 Inside Out of Passing

BACK ROLL TECHNIQUE

Contact the ball with leaning forward posture and change the platform angle without any arm action to produce the correct reflection angle. With this method, the passer spontaneously falls backwards after the ball contacts the passers platform. The back roll technique is a very effective technique and is most used when passing top spin serves with high velocity.

Front View and Side View of the Back Roll Technique (Tara Cross-Battle, USA)

BENDING ELBOW TECHNIQUE

This technique needs perfect execution, such as timing, elbow angle, point of contact, and a solid foundation. In the series below, #11 Miyuki Takahashi from Japan, bends her elbows slightly as she contacts the ball (picture 2&3), then draws her platform back towards her Tanden (picture 4). Pay specific attention to the stability of her lower body. Her ankles and knees are bent sufficiently and her knees are in front of her toes.

Bend Elbow Technique by Miyuki Takahashi, Japan

136 Inside Out of Passing

PASS-SET TECHNIQUE

PASS SET DRILL

Execution: The coach tosses or attacks at the passer. The passer must dig the ball to self and set the ball high to a target at the antenna.

Purpose of the drill: To control the speed of the ball. This drill also helps passers understand platform control and the ability to prevent the overpass. A player can learn how to put the ball straight up in the air naturally by practicing this drill.

Toshi Yoshida & Tara Cross-Battle, USA

Chapter 4: Drills **137**

Toshi Yoshida & Tara Cross-Battle, USA

DON'T LET THE BALL DROP!

This is the worst passing mistake. This problem has nothing to do with the mechanics of passing. My idea is for our passers to (at least) put the ball up in the air and give our setter and hitters a chance to attack the ball.

Cause #1: High velocity

The velocity of serving is so high that sometimes players may not be able to touch the ball, especially in the case of a jump top-spin serve with high velocity that travels to the passer's side above their waist. If the passer cannot quickly get in the right position to pass, they will either be hit by the serve, swing their arms, shank the ball, or bend themselves backward to let the ball go.

For high velocity serves, the passers:

NEED quicker reaction time (explosive power), better prediction and flexibility.

Cause #2: Sudden change of the flight trajectory

The ball sinks in front of the player or curves drastically due to altitude or ventilation of the gym. The passers:

NEED quicker reaction time (explosive power) and to improve muscle strength.

Cause #3: Wrong judgment

Even though the tempo is slow and easy to pass, sometimes a player just lets the ball drop. The minute the ball is served, the passer must be able to predict whether it is in or out. The passers:

> **NEED** *better prediction focus and concentration.*
> *(See the Serve on pgs. 15-17)*

Cause #4: System problem

The ball drops between players because the players don't know their areas of responsibility. The coach:

> **NEEDS** *to develop the path for the players*

NOW WE NEED TO LOOK INTO TEAM PASSING.

CHAPTER 5

Team Passing

1. Path of Players
2. Patterns
   a. Patterns in the World
   b. A look at the World
      (China, Cuba, Russia)
3. Team Passing Drills

Ball control is the key to success. Competition in the world is tough.

Team USA has a lot to do and will continue to work hard to get there.

USA Women's National Team at the World Championships, September 2002.

Chapter 5: Team Passing **141**

PATH OF PLAYERS

The path of players must be decided by the coach! It is absolutely important for players to know their responsible area to pass and the path of movement.

DECIDING FACTORS: PATH OF MOVEMENT

1. Basic path is based on the serve
2. Serve receive pattern
3. Pass-hitter's position
4. Passing range of the individual: The range of movement of your players is limited. Each player has a strong and a weak side in moving as well as one leg that will be stronger than the other. Training for passing range will depend on individual athleticism and injury. Very few players have equal muscle strength and equal strong sides to pass. Usually if the right leg is stronger, the player's right side will also be their stronger passing side.

BASIC IDEA: PATH OF PLAYERS MOVEMENT

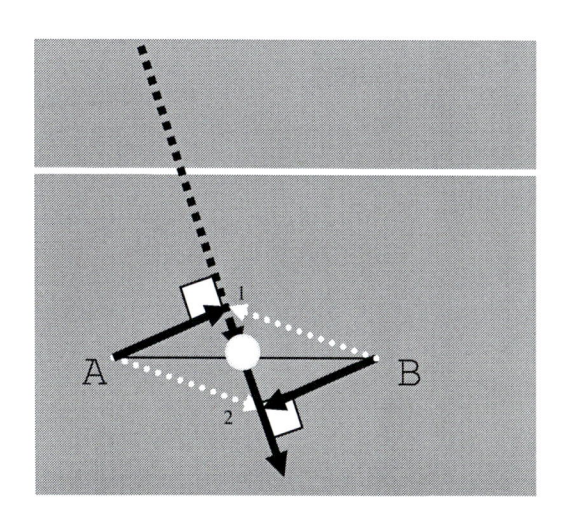

The distance from player A to 1 is shorter than the distance from player B to 1. If player A were to pass the ball at 2, player A would have to follow the balls movement which is a more difficult skill. Therefore, player A should cut off the angle of the ball to pass the ball at 1 while player B would pass the ball at 2. Player A moves in front of player B and player B moves behind player A. This is the basic idea originating from geometry.

The next question is which of the players should pass the ball at the white circle or what I call the 'grey area.' The answer is very simple. The basic theory should be utilized in this case as well. Player A should move in front of player B in order to pass the ball coming to the grey area.

This is a basic path based upon what I just mentioned but for 3 passers in serve receive.

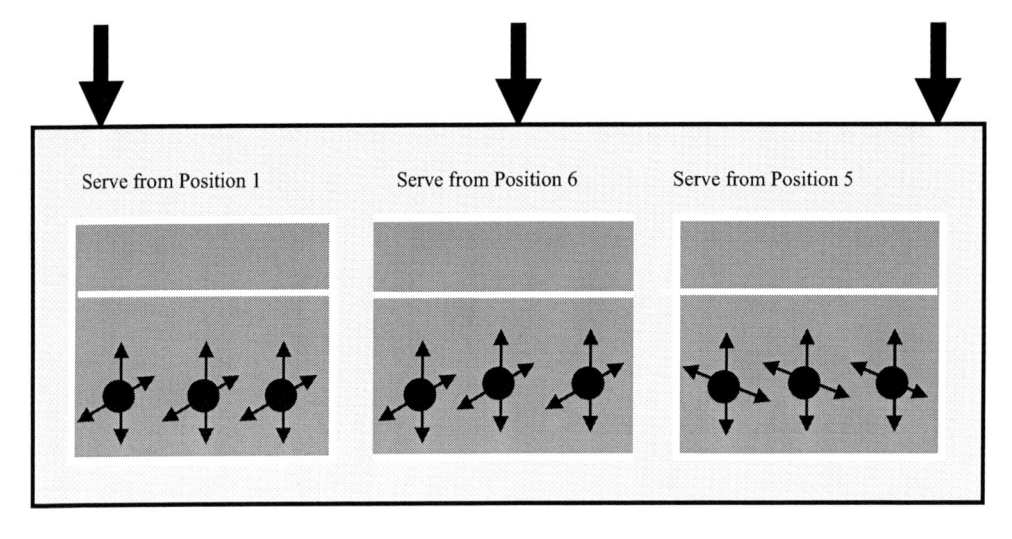

Serve from Position 1

Serve from Position 6

Serve from Position 5

Chapter 5: Team Passing **143**

PASSING PATH OF PLAYERS

In my USA system, I prefer that the pass-hitter does not go behind.

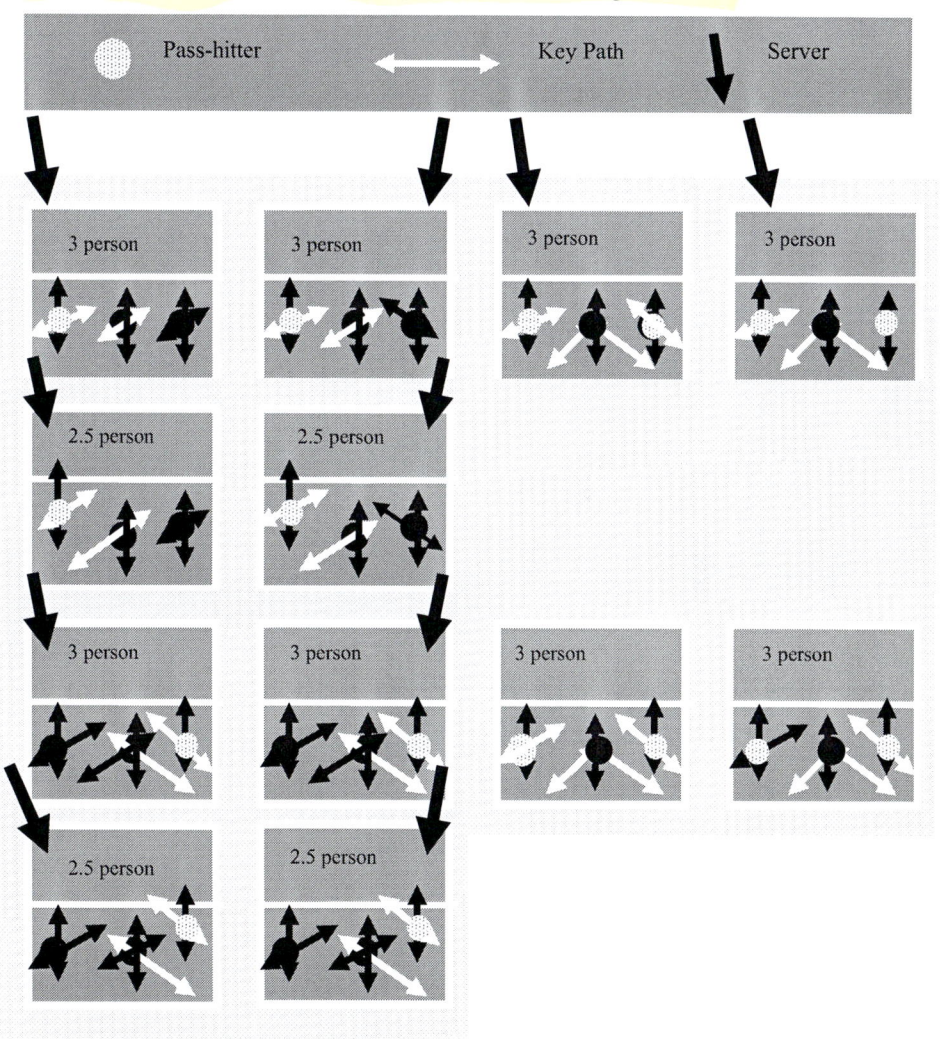

Pass-hitter	Key Path	Server

3 person
3 person
3 person
3 person

2.5 person
2.5 person

3 person
3 person
3 person
3 person

2.5 person
2.5 person

OTHER FACTORS FOR THE PATH

1. Sharing Responsibilities

This is a common approach to passing. Player A and B pass in designated areas. Even though Player A is a hitter, A has to stay until they are sure that the serve does not come into the area that they have to cover. If Player A has decent passing skills, it would be good for A to reduce Player B's area of responsibility.

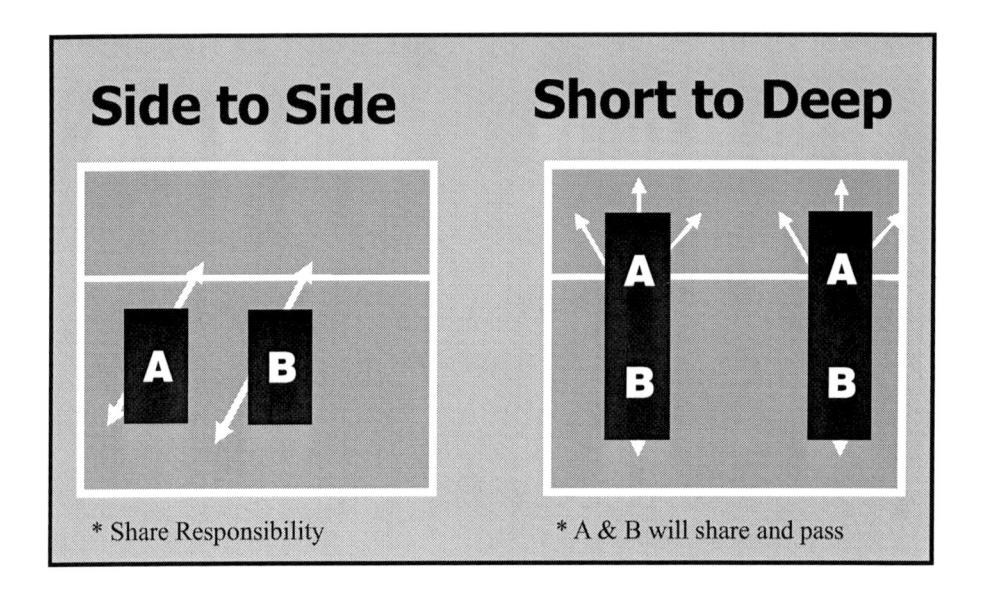

Side to Side

* Share Responsibility

Short to Deep

* A & B will share and pass

2. "Show & Take" Passing Responsibility

This is a unique system to serve receive pass in. Player A does not pass and goes to the location where A has to go to approach as the serve is hit. Player B passes the ball in front and behind Player A in the position 4 area. If Player A is the middle hitter that has responsibility of a first tempo attack, then this movement would be good but Player B would have a larger area to cover. We are deceiving because it looks like Player A passes, but Player A does not.

Chapter 5: Team Passing **145**

Side to Side

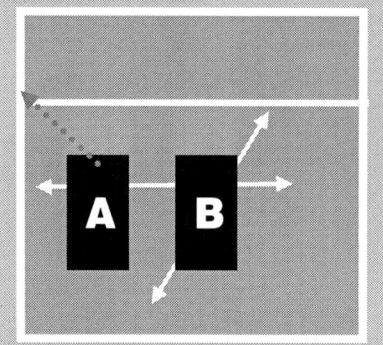

Player A leaves the area and Player B passes A's area.

Short to Deep

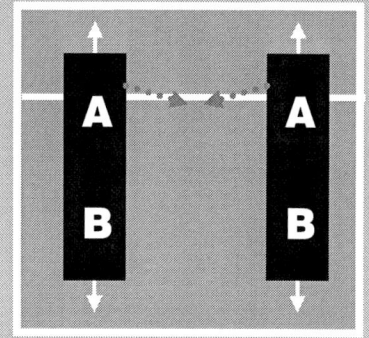

Player A does not pass. A moves out of the way for Player B to pass.

PATTERNS

There are many possible passing patterns for your team. The coach must decide which one is the best for the team.

DECIDING FACTOR OF PATTERNS

Personnel

How many passers do you have? Who can pass well? How do they pass? Those are basic questions. Below, I have offered some keys for patterns in relation to the number of passers you may have. The fewer players in a pattern, the easier it is for the players to understand the path but the more area the players have to cover. The more players in a pattern, the more difficult it is for the players to understand the path, but the less area there is for each passer to cover.

Relationship with offense

The combination of a first ball side out attack off of a serve receive ball and the serve reception pattern are closely related to one another.

Serving

The tendencies of the serve would be a major consideration in making the decision on who is passing. You would be able to pass any kind of serve with a pattern that is less confusing. However, with an easier pattern, you may have to have more than three people to pass the high velocity top-spin serve.

Chapter 5: Team Passing **147**

PATTERNS IN THE WORLD

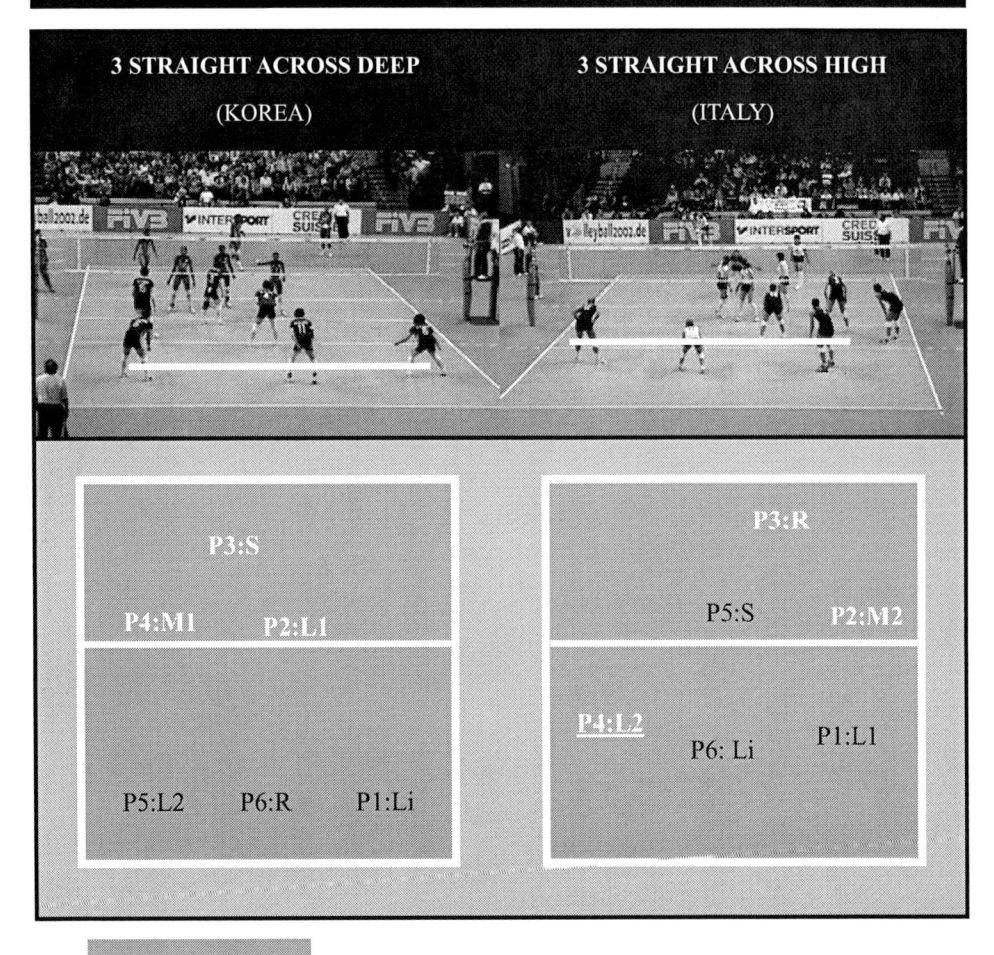

3 STRAIGHT ACROSS DEEP
(KOREA)

3 STRAIGHT ACROSS HIGH
(ITALY)

P3:S

P4:M1   P2:L1

P5:L2   P6:R   P1:Li

P3:R

P5:S   P2:M2

P4:L2
         P6: Li   P1:L1

P4	P3	P2
P5	P6	P1

LEGEND

Li: Libero

S: Setter

M: Middle

L: Left

R: Right

Underline: Pass-hitter

148 Inside Out of Passing

3 ACROSS HIGH "V" (RUSSIA)	EXTREME PATTERN OF 3 ACROSS HIGH "V" (RUSSIA)
P3:L2 　　P2:M1 　　　P1:S **P4:R** 　　　P6:L1 　　P5:Li　(Back row attack)	P3:S P4:M1　　　　　　P1:Li 　**P2:L1** 　　　　　　P6: R 　　　P5:L2 (does not pass)

P4	P3	P2
P5	P6	P1

LEGEND

Li: Libero

S: Setter

M: Middle

L: Left

R: Right

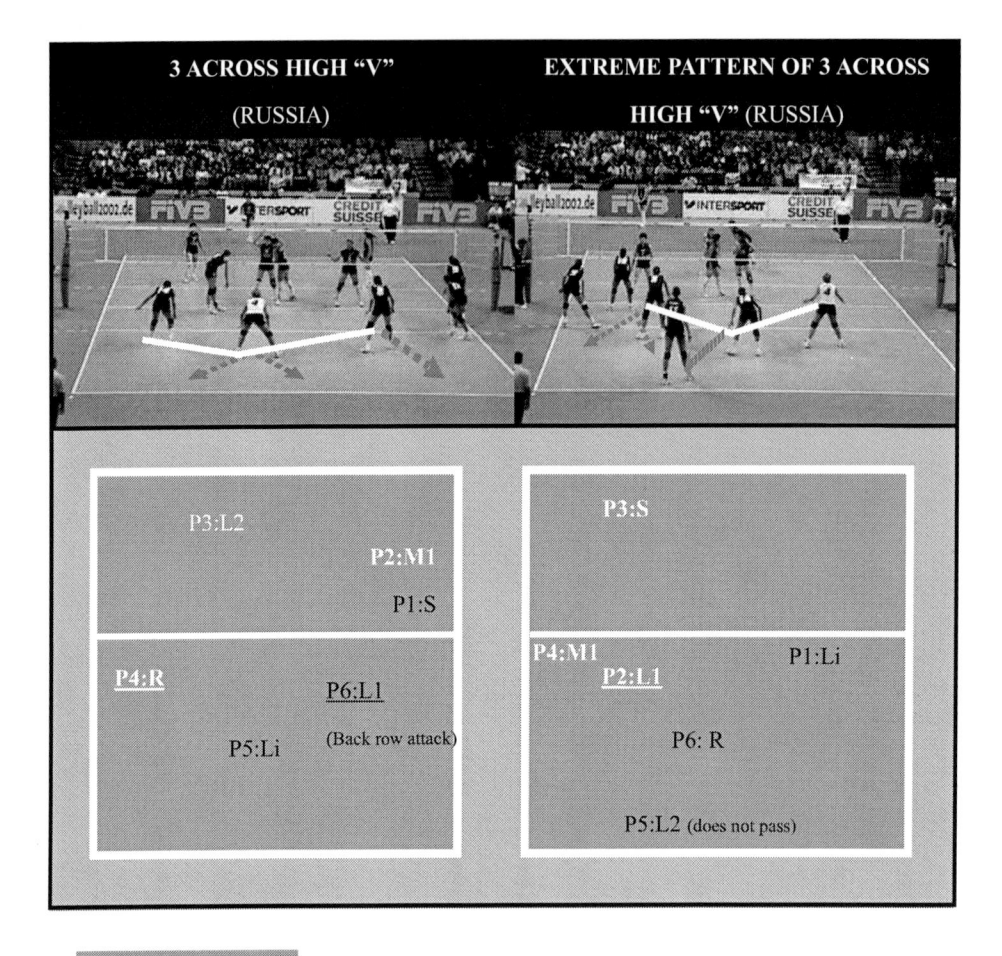

Underline: Pass-hitter

Chapter 5: Team Passing **149**

| 2.5 "L" (CHINA) | 2.5 REVERSE "L" (ITALY) |

The libero covers half of the court.

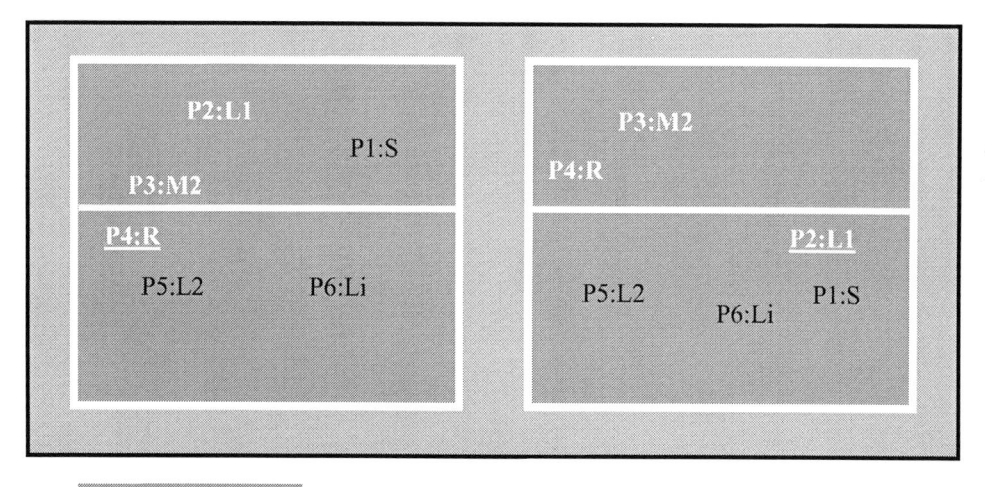

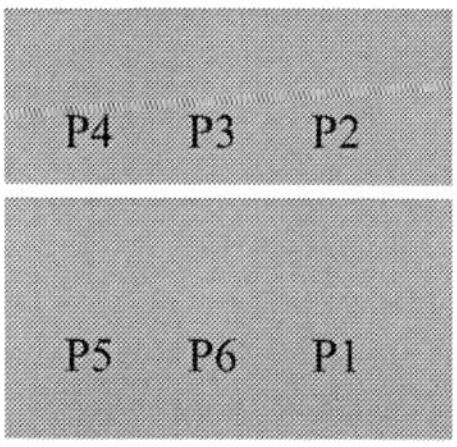

P2:L1			P3:M2		
P3:M2		P1:S	P4:R		
P4:R					P2:L1
P5:L2		P6:Li	P5:L2	P6:Li	P1:S

P4	P3	P2
P5	P6	P1

LEGEND

Li: Libero

S: Setter

M: Middle

L: Left

R: Right

Underline: Pass-hitter

150 Inside Out of Passing

4 TRAPEZOID

(CUBA)

4 ACROSS VS. JUMP TOP SPIN SERVE

(JAPAN)

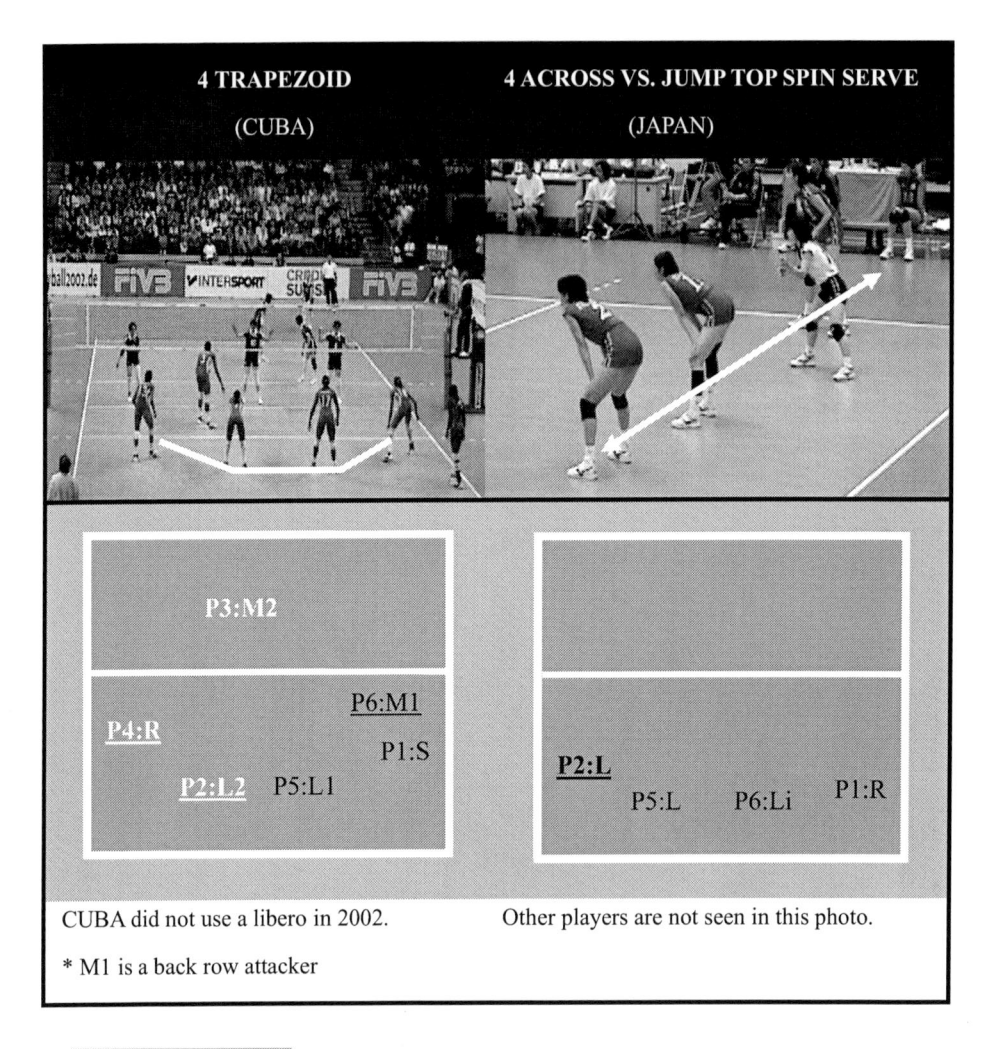

P3:M2	
P4:R P6:M1 P1:S P2:L2 P5:L1	P2:L P5:L P6:Li P1:R

CUBA did not use a libero in 2002.

* M1 is a back row attacker

Other players are not seen in this photo.

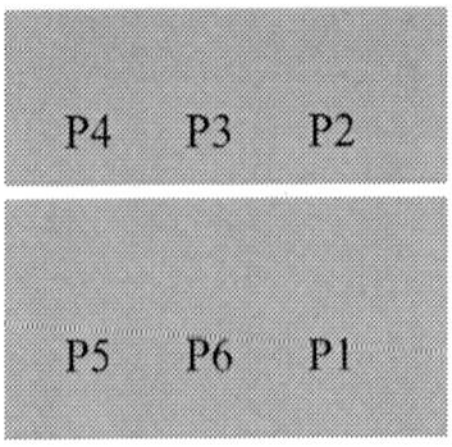

P4	P3	P2
P5	P6	P1

LEGEND

Li: Libero

S: Setter

M: Middle

L: Left

R: Right

Underline: Pass-hitter

Chapter 5: Team Passing **151**

"W"
(Korea)

"N"
(Japan)

		P4:S			
	P3:R	P3:M1			
P4:M1	P5:S P2:L1	P2:L1		P1:R	
	P6: Li P1:M2	P5:L2		P6:Li	

P4	P3	P2
P5	P6	P1

LEGEND

Li: Libero

S: Setter

M: Middle

L: Left

R: Right

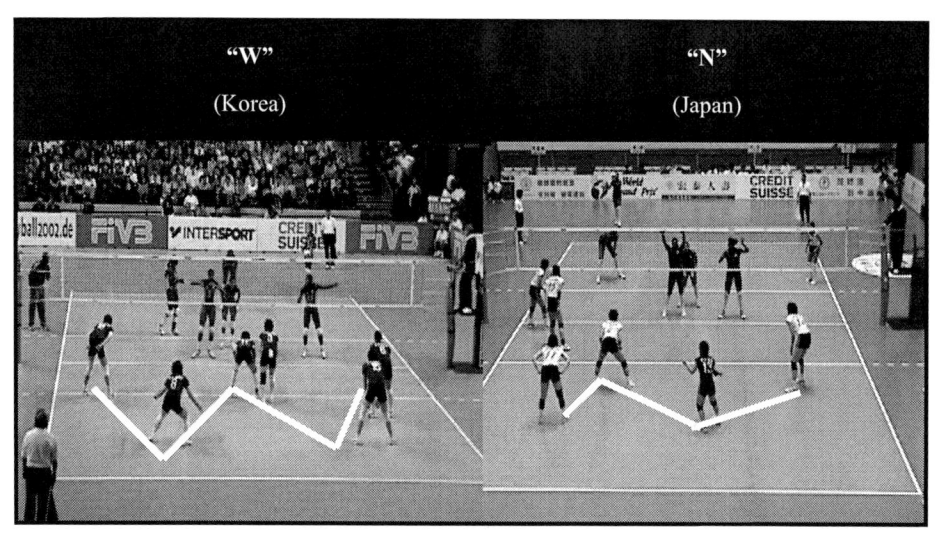

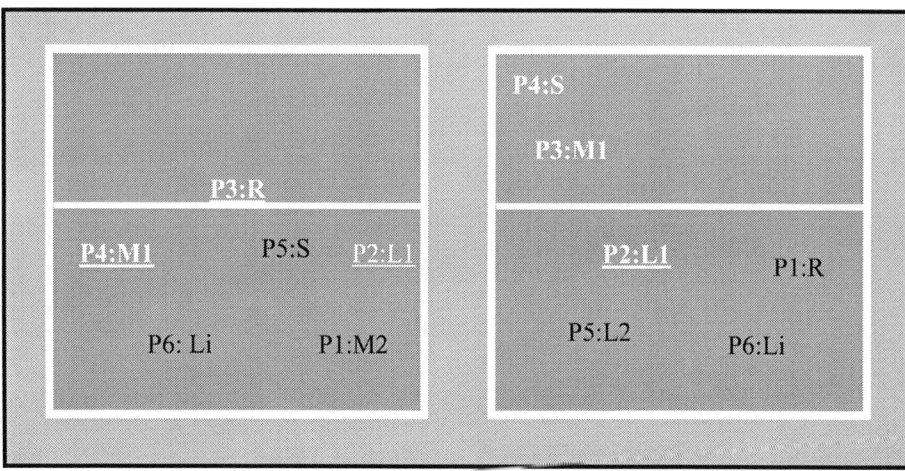

Underline: Pass-hitter

TEAM PASSING DRILLS

COACHES SHOULD......

1) Make a decision on the patterns and the path of players (not only side-to-side but also short and deep responsibilities).
2) Work on the path with short distance serving (Drill 1) to regular distance (Drill 2) from different angles.
3) Work on breaking down group passing with at least two passers in many different ways.
4) Work on team passing with many players in that pattern.

DRILL #1: THROW BALL "X" PATTERNS

Chapter 5: Team Passing **153**

Tara Cross-Battle & Cynthia Barboza, USA

Chapter 5: Team Passing **155**

DRILL #2 WITH SERVE

156 Inside Out of Passing

Tara Cross-Battle & Cynthia Barboza, USA

TEAM PASSING PROGRESSION

3 ACROSS PLUS

4 TRAPEZOID

"W"

1) SIDE TO SIDE
Start training with 2 to 3 players to work on relationships.

2) FRONT TO BACK
Work on relationships with the MB and their front to back reaction.

3) TOGETHER
Put the entire passing system together.

● = Passers

● = Front Row Pass-hitters

Arrows are examples of movement

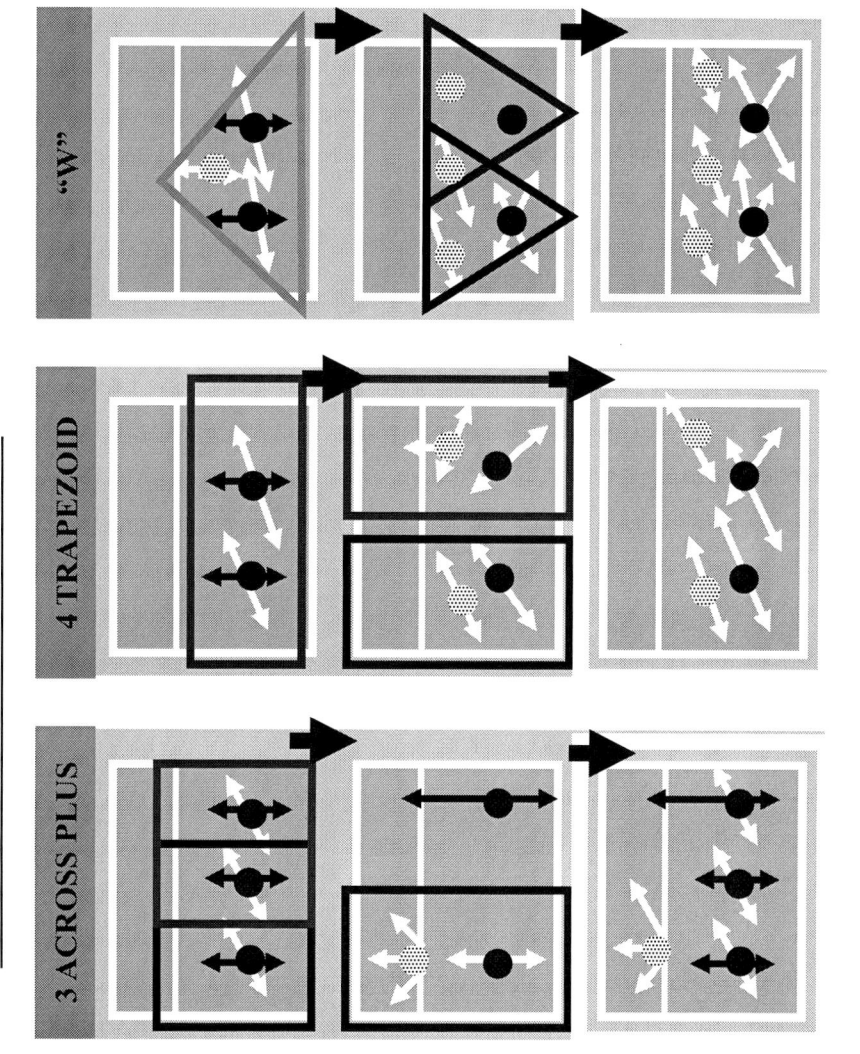

CHAPTER 6

Passing Patterns Around the World

I know that many coaches in the United States are very good at creating their own distinguished passing patterns. However, I think it is still very important for coaches to become knowledgeable about international, team passing patterns as well. We will take a look at China and Russia, who were the top two passing teams at the 2002 World Championships, according to the FIVB (Federation International De Volleyball) passing statistics and Cuba, the only team in the world using a 6-2. In addition, China took 1st place at the 2004 Olympic Games in Athens, Greece with Russia and Cuba finishing in 2nd and 3rd place respectively.

160 Inside Out of Passing

Case Study of China
2.5 & 3 across (2002)

STARTING LINE UP

R	M2	L1
L2	M1	S

China uses the "hands on knees posture" as their ready posture and elbows back in "Go Posture". Chinese passers have been trained to pass the ball in the center of their body as often as they can. This is what I call Tanden passing. They all have good timing, a good feel for the ball and great platforms. Chinese players are also very skilled with their hands. In most cases, even if the serve is tough, they can manage to make a good miss instead of getting aced. Some passing techniques include: Foot position- Chinese passers are taught to square to the target every time. When Chinese passers are in Position 1, they will start with their left foot forward.

©V-spirit.com

Pass Hitters (PH) are Lefts, Rights, and Middles. Liberos often pass for the middles and lefts. China uses a 2.5 passing pattern in rotations 1 in order to take advantage of their most mobile, front row pass hitters. They use a 3 person across pattern in rotations 2, 3, 4, 5, and 6. The right player is a dynamic and mobile pass-hitter and a good representation of Chinese skills. The Chinese offense is also very fast so transition movement from passing to hitting is very quick.

Chapter 6: Passing Patterns Around the World **161**

Case Study of China
R1- 2.5 Across

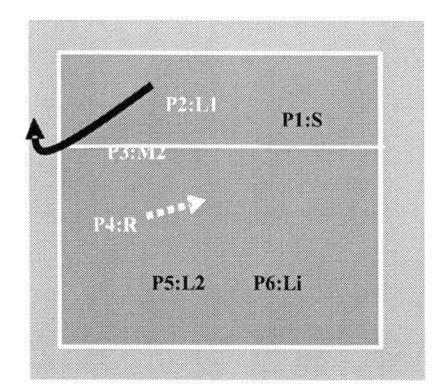

[Diagram showing court positions: P2:L1, P1:S, P3:M2, P4:R, P5:L2, P6:Li]

China starts with 2.5 passers in serve receive with a libero, a left, and a right side PH in the formation. The libero is in for a middle attacker and covers half of the court. The left in P2 does not pass and moves towards P4 to attack.

*Players in white are designated in the front row.

ROTATION 1
COMBO #1

Phase 1: On servers contact.

Phase 2: P6:Li passes the ball while P2:L1 moves outside of the court.

Phase 3: (As the setter touches the ball): P3:M2 runs a quick approach at the setter and P4:R runs a slide approach.

Phase 4: (P4 as hitting) P3:M2 attacks a quick behind the setter.

Chapter 6: Passing Patterns Around the World   **163**

ROTATION 1
COMBO #2

Phase 1: On servers contact.

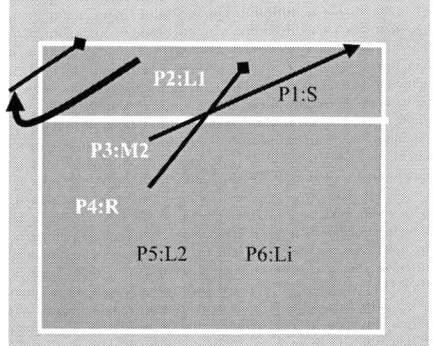

Phase 2: P5:L2 passes the ball while P2:L1 moves outside of the court. P3:M2 stays in front of the setter.

Phase 3: The setter touches the ball and P4:R runs the slide.

Phase 4: P4:R attacks the slide.

164 Inside Out of Passing

Case Study of China
R2- 3 Across

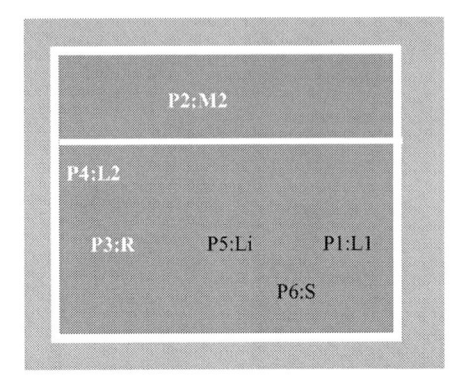

```
        P2:M2
    P4:L2
  P3:R      P5:Li       P1:L1
                P6:S
```

Now they have the L2 in the front row. They pass 3 across with the libero and the right side PH plus the front row left side hitter (L2). P3:R plays the important PH role, while the libero passes for a middle attacker in the middle of the court.

Chapter 6: Passing Patterns Around the World **165**

ROTATION 2
COMBO #1

Phase 1: On Servers Contact

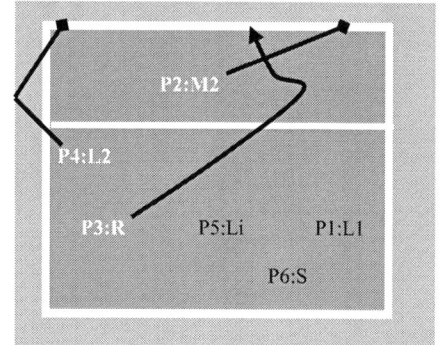

Phase 2: P1:L1 passes the ball. P3:R and P2:M2 are moving toward the setter. P4:L2 is already outside of the court.

Phase 3: P2:M2 is ready to jump behind the setter while P3:R is faking to go behind the setter.

Phase 4: P2:M goes for a slide and P3:R attacks out of the middle.

166 Inside Out of Passing

ROTATION 2
COMBO #2

Phase 1: On servers contact.

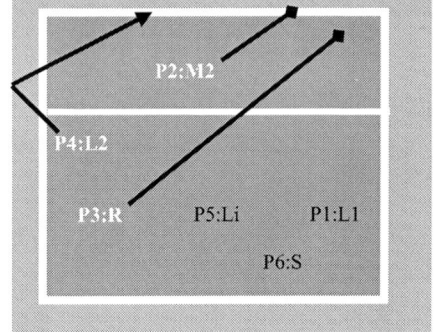

Phase 2: P5:Li passes the ball and P4:L2 moves outside of the court.

Phase 3: P2:M2 is jumping behind the setter while P3:R is still in front of the setter.

Phase 4: P4:L attacks a set in zone 3 while both P2:M2 and P3:R are behind the setter.

Chapter 6: Passing Patterns Around the World **167**

Case Study of China
R3- 3 Across

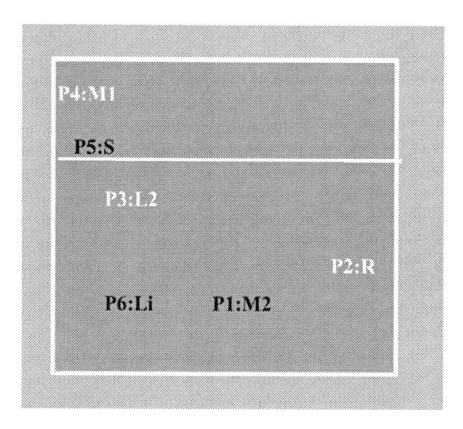

P4:M1	
P5:S	
P3:L2	
	P2:R
P6:Li P1:M2	

This is a typical 3 across serve receive pattern with a libero, a middle in the backrow, and a right side (PH) in the front row. In this rotation, the libero passes for the left side hitter along with the middle.

168 Inside Out of Passing

ROTATION 3
COMBO #1

Phase 1: On servers contact.

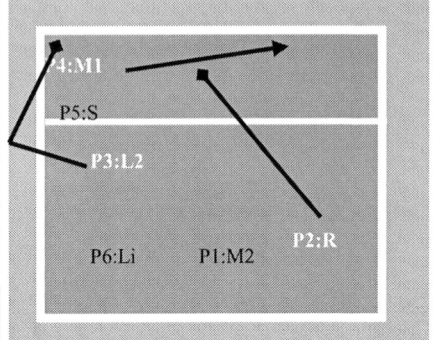

```
4:M1
P5:S
P3:L2
P6:Li    P1:M2    P2:R
```

Phase 2: P1:M2 passes the ball while P3:L2 moves outside of the court.

Phase 3: P4:M1 runs a quick set behind the setter and P2:R runs a set in front of the setter.

Phase 4: P4:M1 attacks the quick set behind the setter.

Chapter 6: Passing Patterns Around the World **169**

ROTATION 3
COMBO #2

Phase 1: On servers contact.

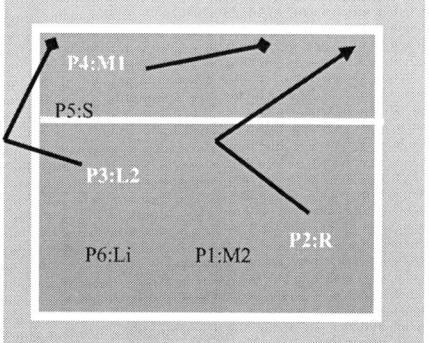

Phase 2: P2:R passes the ball. P3:L2 is already outside of the court for the outside set.

Phase 3: P4:M1 runs a quick set behind the setter. P2:R moves to the middle of the court and changes the direction of her approach.

Phase 4: P2:R attacks the slide.

170 Inside Out of Passing

Case Study of China
R4- 3 Across

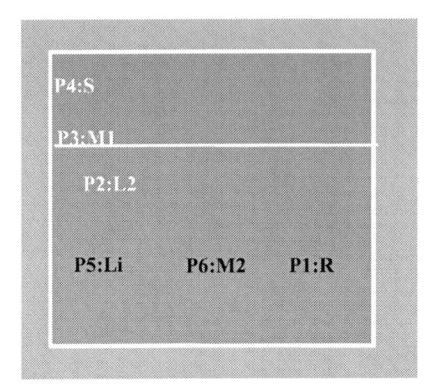

P4:S		
P3:M1		
P2:L2		
P5:Li	P6:M2	P1:R

This is a typical 3 across with the libero, middle in the back row, and a right side in the back row.

Chapter 6: Passing Patterns Around the World **171**

ROTATION 4
COMBO #1

Phase 1: On servers contact.

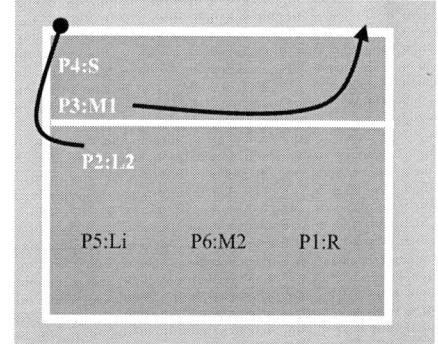

```
P4:S
P3:M1
P2:L2

P5:Li    P6:M2    P1:R
```

Phase 2: P1:R passes the ball. P2:L2 is already outside of the court for the outside set.

Phase 3: P3:M1 runs the slide.

Phase 4: P3:M1 attacks the slide.

172 Inside Out of Passing

ROTATION 4
COMBO #2

Phase 1: On servers contact.

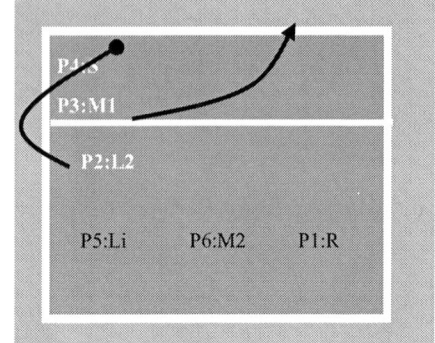

Phase 2: P5:Li passes the ball while P2:L2 moves outside of the court.

Phase 3: P2:L2 runs a second tempo set in the zone 3 area. P3:M1 is about to jump for a quick attack.

Phase 4: P3:M1 attacks the quick set behind the setter.

Chapter 6: Passing Patterns Around the World **173**

Case Study of China
R5- 3 Across

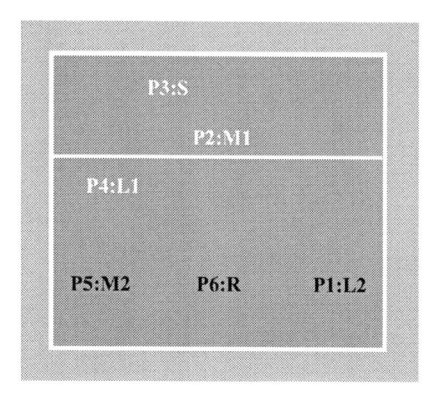

```
              P3:S
                  P2:M1
   P4:L1

   P5:M2    P6:R    P1:L2
```

In this rotation, the L1 is up. The typical 3 across with a middle, right and left in the back row. There is no libero in this rotation.

174 Inside Out of Passing

ROTATION 5
COMBO #1

Phase 1: On servers contact.

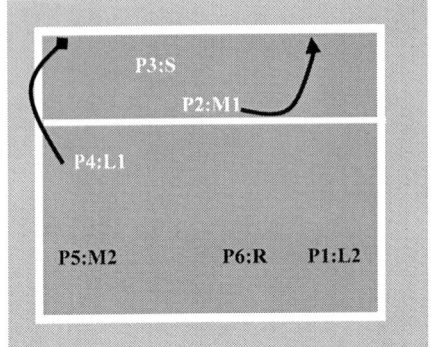

```
         P3:S
              P2:M1
P4:L1

P5:M2      P6:R    P1:L2
```

Phase 2: P6:R passes the ball while P2:L1 moves outside of the court.

Phase 3: P2:M1 runs past the setter.

Phase 4: P2:M1 attacks a slide.

Chapter 6: Passing Patterns Around the World **175**

ROTATION 5
COMBO #2

Phase 1: On servers contact.

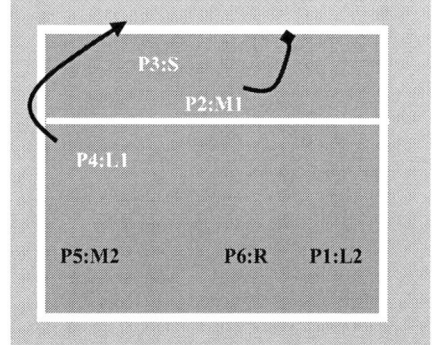

Phase 2: P5:M2 passes the ball while P4:L1 moves outside the court.

Phase 3: P2:M1 runs past the setter.

Phase 4: P4:L1 attacks a set in zone 3.

176 Inside Out of Passing

Case Study of China
R6- 3 Across

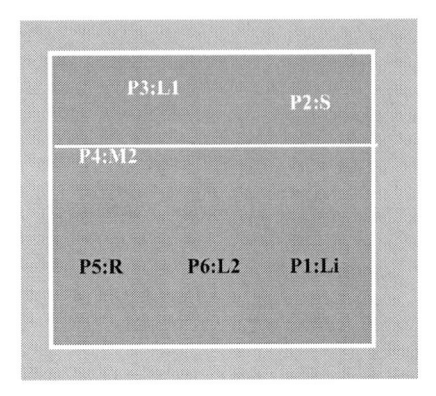

P3:L1		P2:S
P4:M2		
P5:R	P6:L2	P1:Li

In Rotation 6, the middle is up with a typical 3 across formation. A right, left and libero, who passes for a middle, are the 3 serve receive passers.

ROTATION 6
COMBO #1 Blue

Phase 1: On servers contact.

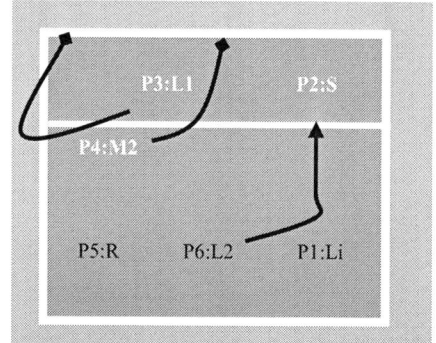

Phase 2: P1:Li passes the ball and P3:L1 moves outside of the court.

Phase 3: P4:M2 runs in front of the setter and P6:L2 moves behind the P1:Li to prepare a back row attack.

Phase 4: P6:L2 attacks from the back row on the right side (attacks what we call a blue set).

178 Inside Out of Passing

ROTATION 6
COMBO #2

Phase 1: On servers contact.

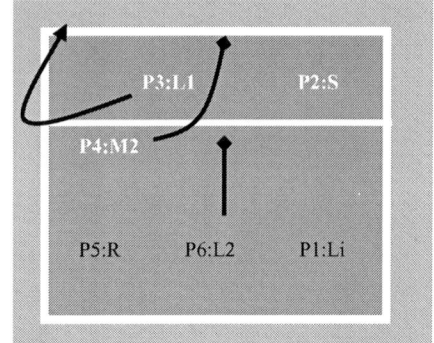

Phase 2: P5:R passes the ball while P3:L1 moves outside of the court.

Phase 3: P4:M2 runs a quick in front of the setter while P6:L2 goes for a back row attack out of position 6 or what I call a white.

Phase 4: P3:L1 attacks an outside set at the antennae.

Chapter 6: Passing Patterns Around the World **179**

Case Study of Cuba
6-2 System (2002)

**STARTING
LINE UP**

Setter leads Left

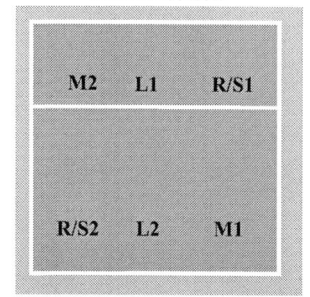

M2	L1	R/S1
R/S2	L2	M1

R/S= Right Side Hitter & Setter

Cuba was the only team in the world in 2002 that used a 6-2 system without a libero. The Cuban pass hitters are equally skilled, so they do not need a libero as a substitute. Cuba has been using a 4 person trapezoid as the basic serve receive formation for years.

Set/Hit players pass the ball well. Their approaches are very dynamic. For Cuba, these are their best all around players who play the most important role for them. Cuba also uses their middles to pass the ball in serve receive.

180 Inside Out of Passing

Case Study of Cuba
R6- 4 Trapezoid

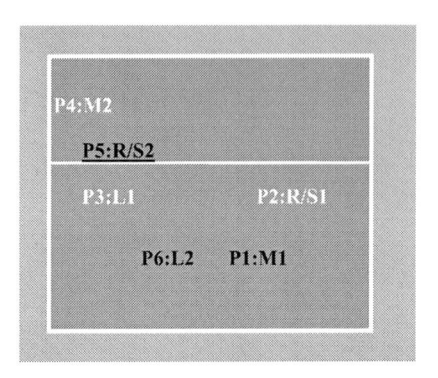

P4:M2		
P5:R/S2		
P3:L1		P2:R/S1
	P6:L2 P1:M1	

Cuba starts in rotation 6 and places the front row left and R/S in a 4 trapezoid with the back row middle and left side. P1:M1 will attack from the back row.

Players in white are designated in the front row and the setter is underlined.

Chapter 6: Passing Patterns Around the World **181**

ROTATION 6
COMBO #1

Phase 1: On servers contact.

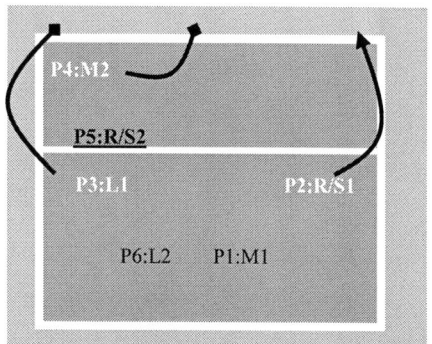

P4:M2

P5:R/S2

P3:L1   P2:R/S1

P6:L2   P1:M1

Phase 2: P3:L1 passes the ball.

Phase 3: P4:M2 runs in front of the setter. P3:L1 moves outside of the court and P2:R/S1 runs a back set.

Phase 4: P2:R/S1 attacks a back set.

182 Inside Out of Passing

ROTATION 6
COMBO #2

Phase 1: On servers contact.

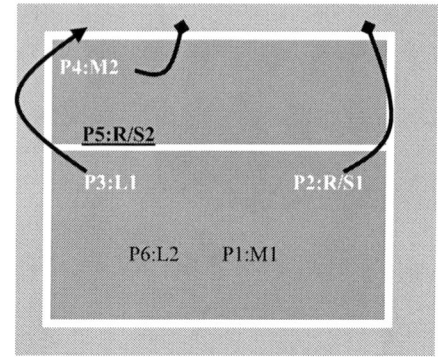

```
P4:M2
     P5:R/S2
P3:L1              P2:R/S1

     P6:L2   P1:M1
```

Phase 2: P1:M1 passes the ball while P3:L1 moves outside of the court.

Phase 3: P4:M2 runs a set in zone 3 and the P2:R/S1 prepares for a right side set.

Phase 4: P3:L1 attacks an outside set.

Chapter 6: Passing Patterns Around the World **183**

Case Study of Cuba
R1- 4 Trapezoid

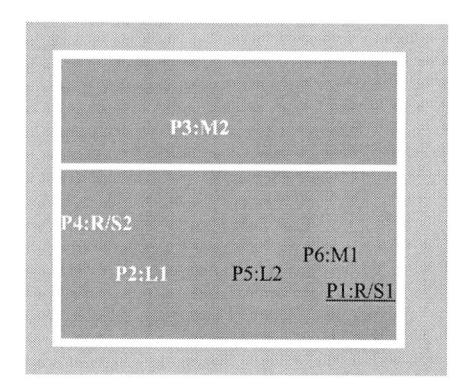

```
                P3:M2

P4:R/S2
                          P6:M1
        P2:L1    P5:L2
                          P1:R/S1
```

In Rotation 1, they are in a 4 trapezoid with the front row left and right side along with the backrow left and middle. P6:M1 will attack from the backrow.

184 Inside Out of Passing

ROTATION 1
COMBO #1

Phase 1: On servers contact.

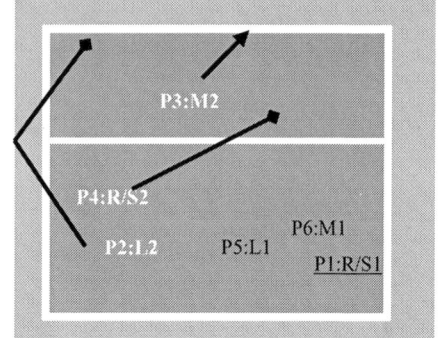

Phase 2: P4:R/S2 passes the ball.

Phase 3: P2:L2 moves outside of the court. P5:M1 runs a quick in front of the setter and P4:R/S2 runs a slide.

Phase 4: P5:M1 attacks the quick in front of the setter.

Chapter 6: Passing Patterns Around the World   **185**

ROTATION 1
COMBO #2

Phase 1: On servers contact.

```
           P3:M2
  P4:R/S2
                        P6:M1
  P2:L1    P5:L2
                        P1:R/S1
```

Phase 2: P6:M2 passes the ball.

Phase 3: P2:L1 moves outside of the court while P3:M2 runs a quick in front of the setter and P4:R/S2 runs a slide.

Phase 4: P3:M2 attacks a quick in zone 3.

186 Inside Out of Passing

Case Study of Cuba
R2- 4 Trapezoid

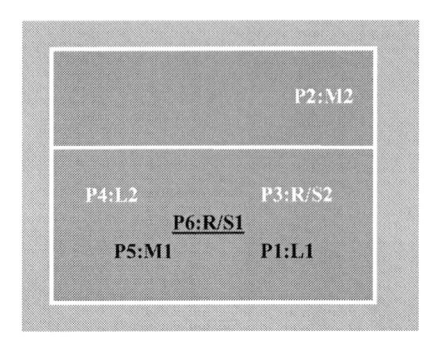

	P2:M2
P4:L2	P3:R/S2
P6:R/S1	
P5:M1	P1:L1

In Rotation 2, Cuba is in a 4 trapezoid serve receive with the front row left, R/S and the back row left and middle. P5:M1 attacks from the back row.

Chapter 6: Passing Patterns Around the World **187**

ROTATION 2
COMBO #1

Phase 1: On servers contact.

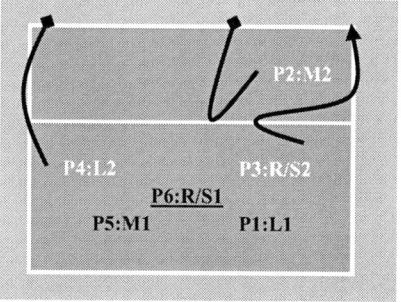

```
                              P2:M2
    P4:L2           P3:R/S1
            P6:R/S1
    P5:M1           P1:L1
```

Phase 2: P1:L1 passes the ball while P4:L2 moves outside of the court.

Phase 3: P2:M2 runs a quick set in front of the setter. P3:R/S2 runs behind the setter.

Phase 4: P3:R/S2 attacks the slide.

188 Inside Out of Passing

ROTATION 2
COMBO #2

Phase 1: On servers contact.

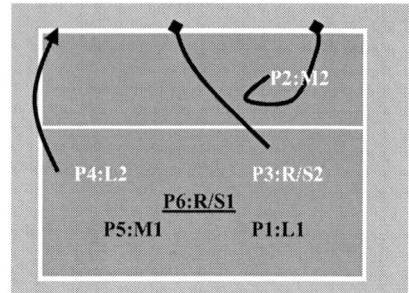

P4:L2		P3:R/S2
	P6:R/S1	
P5:M1		P1:L1

Phase 2: P1:L1 passes the ball while P4:L2 moves outside of the court.

Phase 3: P2:M2 runs a slide and P3:R/S2 runs a second tempo set in front of the setter.

Phase 4: P4:L2 attacks the ball outside.

Chapter 6: Passing Patterns Around the World **189**

Case Study of Cuba
R3- 4 Trapezoid

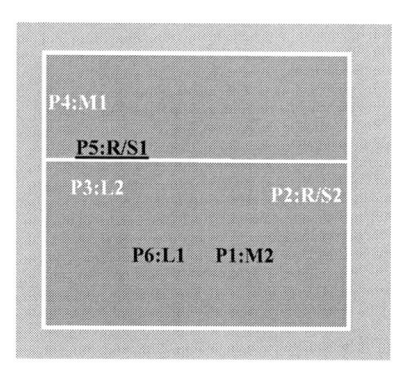

```
P4:M1
P5:R/S1
P3:L2                P2:R/S2
     P6:L1   P1:M2
```

Rotation 3 is a 4 person trapezoid with the front row left, R/S, and the back row left and middle. P1:M2 will attack from the back row. The R3 basic formation is the same as R6 with different players.

ROTATION 3
COMBO #1

Phase 1: On servers contact.

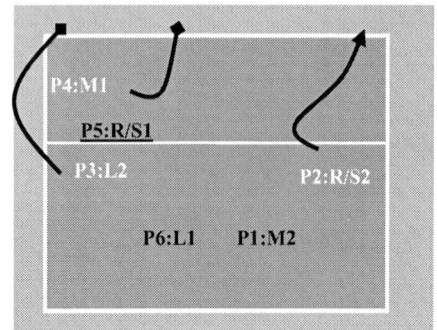

P4:M1		
P5:R/S1		
P3:L2		P2:R/S2
	P6:L1 P1:M2	

Phase 2: P3:L2 passes the ball.

Phase 3: P3:L2 moves outside of the court.

P4:M1 runs a quick in front of the setter.

P2:R/S2 runs a slide.

Phase 4: P2:R/S2 attacks a slide.

Chapter 6: Passing Patterns Around the World **191**

ROTATION 3
COMBO #2

Phase 1: On servers contact.

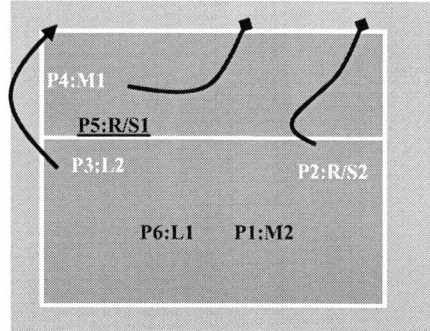

Phase 2: P6:L1 passes the ball while P3:L2 moves outside of the court.

Phase 3: P4:M1 runs a quick in front of the setter. P2:R/S2 runs toward the right side.

Phase 4: P3:L2 attacks at the antennae.

192 Inside Out of Passing

Case Study of Cuba
R4- 4 Trapezoid

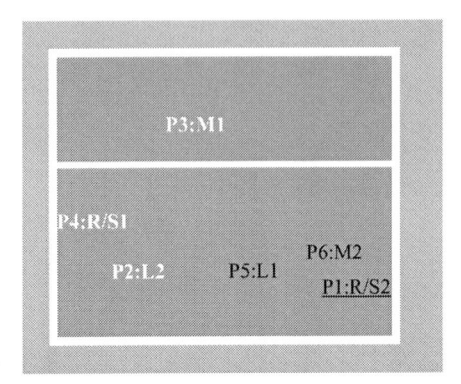

```
                P3:M1

P4:R/S1
                              P6:M2
        P2:L2    P5:L1
                              P1:R/S2
```

Cuba's Rotation 4 is a 4 person trapezoid with the front row left, R/S and the back row middle and left. P6:M2 will attack from the back row. The R4 basic formation is the same as R1 with different players.

Chapter 6: Passing Patterns Around the World   **193**

ROTATION 4
COMBO #1

Phase 1: On servers contact.

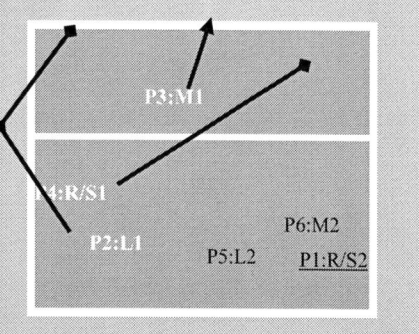

```
         P3:M1
 P4:R/S1
                      P6:M2
    P2:L1   P5:L2     P1:R/S2
```

Phase 2: P4:R/S1 passes the ball.

Phase 3: P2:L2 moves outside of the court. P5:M1 attacks a quick in front of the setter and P4:R/S1 runs a slide.

Phase 4: P3:M1 attacks the quick in front of the setter.

ROTATION 4
COMBO #2

Phase 1: On servers contact.

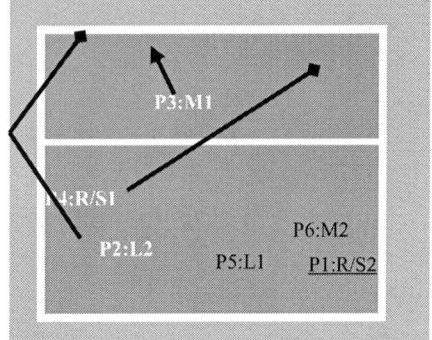

Phase 2: P6:M2 passes the ball.

Phase 3: P2:L1 moves outside of the court while P3:M2 runs a quick in front of the setter and P4:R/S1 runs a slide.

Phase 4: P3:M2 attacks a quick in zone 3.

Chapter 6: Passing Patterns Around the World **195**

Case Study of Cuba
R5- 4 Trapezoid

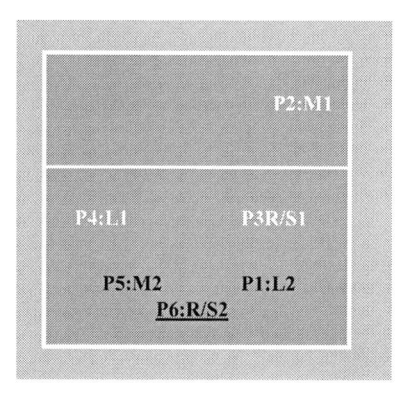

```
                              P2:M1

        P4:L1         P3R/S1

        P5:M2         P1:L2
         P6:R/S2
```

In Rotation 5, Cuba is again in a 4 person trapezoid serve receive with the front row left, R/S and the back row left and middle. P5:M2 is their back row attacker. The R5 basic formation is the same as R2 with different players.

196 Inside Out of Passing

ROTATION 5
COMBO #1

Phase 1: On servers contact.

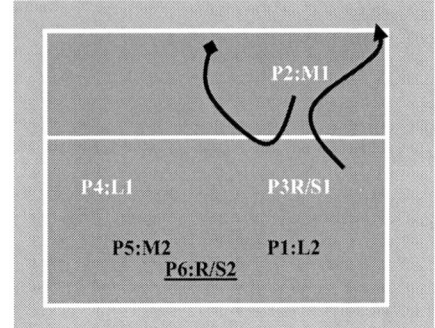

	P2:M1	
P4:L1		P3R/S1
P5:M2	P1:L2	
P6:R/S2		

Phase 2: P4:L1 passes the ball.

Phase 3: P4:L1 finishes her pass. P3:R/S1 runs a slide and P2:M1 runs in front of the setter.

Phase 4: P3:R/S1 attacks the slide.

Case Study of Russia
High 3 Across (2002)

STARTING LINE UP

Setter leads Middle

R	L2	M1
M2	L1	S

Russia is a very good passing team for their height. Here are some characteristics of the Russian style. 1. Sway readiness, 2. Back-Up passing, 3. Wide feet contact, and 4. Low trajectory passing. They all start side-to-side sway movement off of initial readiness posture. They also step back as the server contacts the ball. They try to contact the ball with wide feet and pass the ball from a very low position. This has been their basic style for years.

©V-spirit.com

PH's are Left, Right and Middle. The libero passes for Left and Middle. They start in a very high position on the court especially the PH that passes on the left side of the 3 person. They use a "V" pattern which is a modified basic 3 across. It looks like the deep court serve receive in all rotations is relatively weak, which is sometimes true, but they often use the back-up technique to pass deep court serves.

198 Inside Out of Passing

Case Study of Russia
R1- 3 Across High V

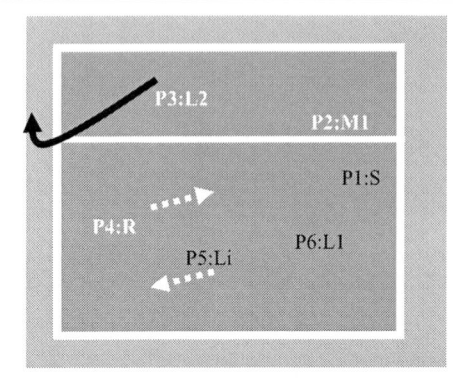

In Rotation 1, Russia is in a "3 Across High V" formation with the Libero and the back row left and right side pass-hitter. The libero helps behind the P4:R. The libero passes for the middle and the P6:L1 hits from the back row.

Chapter 6: Passing Patterns Around the World **199**

ROTATION 1
COMBO #1

Phase 1: On servers contact.

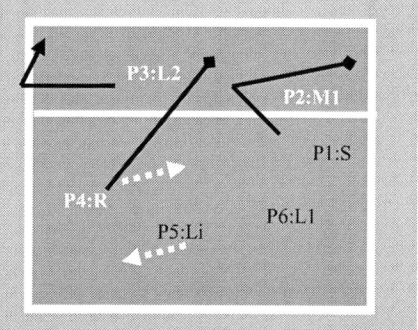

Phase 2: P2:M1 moves in and out in a fake movement. P6:L1 passes the ball while P3:L2 moves outside of the court.

Phase 3: P4:R4 runs a quick in front of the setter while P2:M1 changes the direction of her approach.

Phase 4: P3:L1 attacks an outside set.

ROTATION 1
COMBO #2

Phase 1: On servers contact.

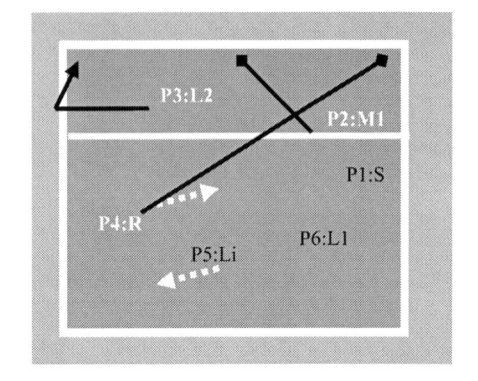

Phase 2: P5:Li passes the ball while P3:L2 moves outside of the court.

Phase 3: P2:M1 runs a quick in front of the setter while P4:R runs the slide behind the setter.

Phase 4: P3:L2 attacks an outside set.

Chapter 6: Passing Patterns Around the World **201**

Case Study of Russia
R2- 3 Across High V

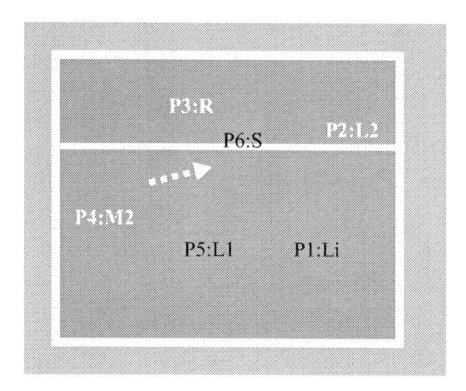

```
        P3:R
    P6:S      P2:L2
P4:M2
    P5:L1    P1:Li
```

In Rotation 2, Russia is in a "3 Across High V" formation with the L1, the front row middle (M2), and the libero passing for the back row middle.

202 Inside Out of Passing

ROTATION 2
COMBO #1

Phase 1: On servers contact.

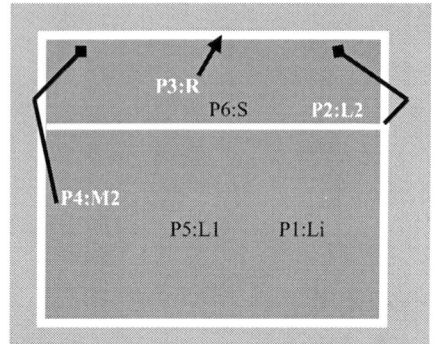

Phase 2: P5:L1 passes the ball while P3:L2 and P4:M2 moves outside of the court.

Phase 3: P3:R runs a quick in front of the setter.

Phase 4: P3:R attacks a quick.

Chapter 6: Passing Patterns Around the World **203**

Case Study of Russia
R3- 3 Across High V

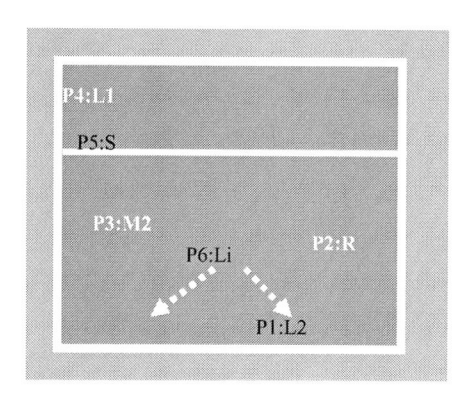

```
P4:L1
  P5:S
     P3:M2
        P6:Li      P2:R
              P1:L2
```

In Rotation 3, Russia is in a "3 Across High V" formation with the libero and the front row middle and right side pass-hitters. The middle in the front row runs a first tempo approach, the libero passes for the back row middle attacker. The libero helps behind the pass-hitters and the left side attacker in the P1 position hits from the back row.

ROTATION 3
COMBO #1

Phase 1: On servers contact.

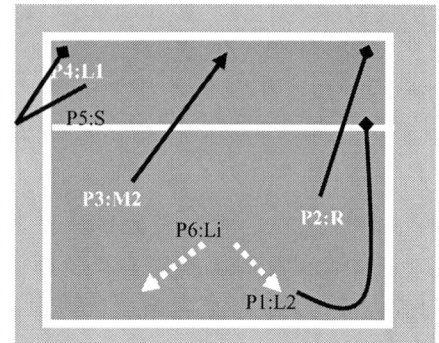

Phase 2: P6:Li passes the ball while P4:L1 moves outside of the court.

Phase 3: P3:M2 runs a quick in front of the setter. P2:R changes the direction of her approach. P1:L2 is ready for a back row attack.

Phase 4: P3:M2 attacks a quick set.

Chapter 6: Passing Patterns Around the World **205**

Case Study of Russia
R4- 3 Across High V

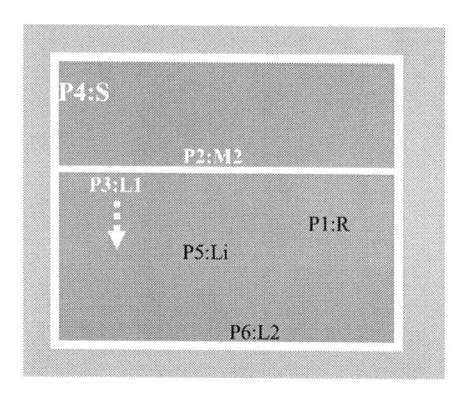

```
P4:S
       P2:M2
P3:L1
  ⋮              P1:R
  ▼     P5:Li

        P6:L2
```

In Rotation 4, Russia is in a "3 Across High V" formation with the libero and right side in the back row. The left side pass-hitter is stacked short. The libero passes for the middle attacker and helps behind the pass-hitters on both sides. The P6:L2 hits from the back row.

ROTATION 4
COMBO #1

Phase 1: On servers contact.

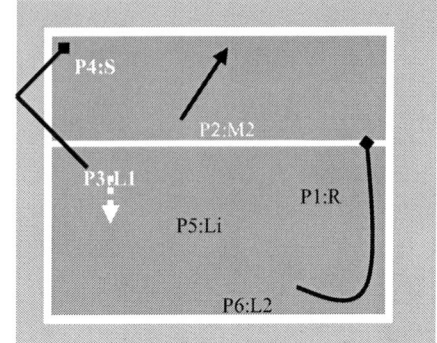

Phase 2: P1:R passes the ball and P3:L1 is trying to move outside of the court. P6:L2 moves to the right side of the court for the back row attack.

Phase 3: P2:M2 runs a quick in front of the setter.

Phase 4: P2:M2 attacks a quick.

Chapter 6: Passing Patterns Around the World **207**

Case Study of Russia
R5- 3 Across High V

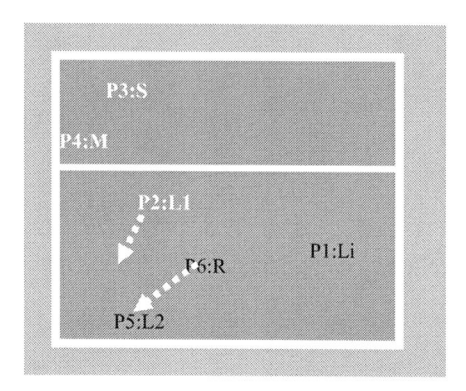

In Rotation 5, Russia is in a "3 Across High V" with the libero and right side in the back row. The left side is a front row pass-hitter. The libero passes for the middle attacker and P6:R helps behind P2:L1. P5:L2 hits out of the back row.

ROTATION 5
COMBO #1

Phase 1: On servers contact.

Phase 2: P2:L1 passes the ball.

Phase 3: P4:M1 is faking a quick set in front of the setter. P2:L1 is trying to move to position 4 for an outside set. P5:L2 is ready for a back row attack.

Phase 4: P4:M1 moves behind the setter and attacks the slide.

Chapter 6: Passing Patterns Around the World **209**

ROTATION 5
COMBO #2

Phase 1: On servers contact.

Phase 2: P6:R passes the ball.

Phase 3: P5:L2 moves to position 1 for what I call a blue set and P4:M1 runs a quick.

Phase 4: P2:L1 attacks an outside set.

210 Inside Out of Passing

Case Study of Russia
R6- 3 Across High V

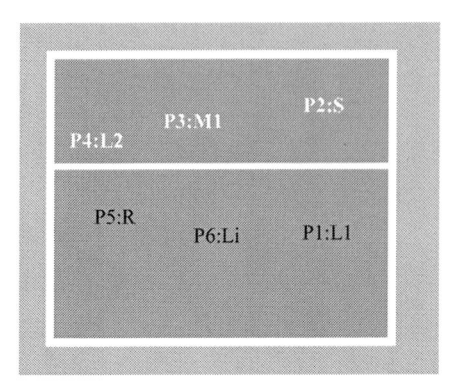

P4:L2	P3:M1	P2:S
P5:R	P6:Li	P1:L1

In Rotation 6, Russia is in a "3 Across High V" formation with the right and left side attackers in the back row. The libero passes for the middle.

Chapter 6: Passing Patterns Around the World **211**

ROTATION 6
COMBO #1

Phase 1: On servers contact.

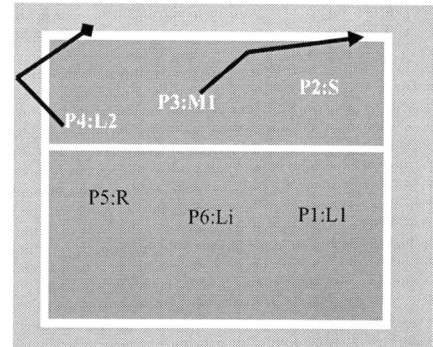

P4:L2	P3:M1	P2:S
P5:R	P6:Li	P1:L1

Phase 2: L6:Li passes the ball and P4:L2 is already outside of the court.

Phase 3: P3:M1 is faking a quick set.

Phase 4: P3:M1 attacks the slide.

CHAPTER 7

5 Minute Drills

LOGAN TOM

(Outside Hitter)

DOB: May 25, 1981

Height: 188 cm

Hometown: Salt Lake City, Utah

Career History:

Club: Klub Boom

College: Stanford University

Professional Teams:

Minas Giras, Brazil (1 year), Monte Schiavo, Italy (1 year)

National Team: 1997- Present

Olympics: 2004, 2000

Quote: "Training under Toshi as a pass-hitter you find how to be patient. For techniques that happen in seconds its hard to see the many different aspects within them. Toshi finds those aspects and breaks them down one by one. Its takes a lot of time and focus but if you're willing to give those to him he can make you into the best pass-hitter you can be."

BASIC 5 MINUTE DRILLS

As coaches, we always feel that we have so many skills and systems we need to improve in order to make a good team. If we only had more time to train! Sometimes individual passing reps are skipped due to the lack of training time. We feel that we need much more time to work on systems in order to prepare for the matches. Obviously, the best drill for preparation is the game itself. Because the game teaches players how to play the uncontrollable parts of a competition, players can rapidly improve skills through playing the game. Understanding all of these ideas, I still encourage you to spend more time improving individual passing skills at every practice, especially younger age players who need adequate repetition in order to produce good habits.

Improving on skills is how we form habits. It usually takes lots of time and repetitions to properly form good habits. However, if you run a drill with the right keys and do it in every practice for a short period of time (3 to 4 weeks), you will see a difference and the habit will be formed. "5 minute drills (5 MD's)" are specific habit forming drills that you do everyday in order to improve your players' skills. Some of the drills in this chapter have already been introduced in earlier chapters but are important habit forming drills. "5 MD's" tell you how to focus on the 8 KEYS and will show a progression that is more practical and can be used in your practice the right way. In your practices, "5 MD's" would only be used as a **segment** of your total passing drills. A "5 MD" can only be implemented in the individual parts of your practice, which is all dependant upon your total training time and the team's needs. Overall, we must remember that we have to keep on doing it to see the results we are looking for. Do it a little bit at every practice to see a change. This can be used as a warm-up in the beginning of practice or a cool-down technique session at the end of practice. Use these drills to reinforce movement and basic passing technique.

5 MD #1: Part of warming up - Movement Drills

1. Without a ball, have players get into "Ready position" and "Go position" upon coach's call.
2. Without a ball, have players get into "Ready" then "Go" and move with shuffle steps in "Go" posture with a simulated ball contact. Have them move side-to-side, forward and back.
3. Have players get into a "Ready" then "Go" posture and make the "Down-up movement" without a ball. Encourage the players to make a full "down" and full "up" movement.
4. You can add other exercises, such as lunges in Chapter 3 or dig and roll techniques, to the warm-up routine as well.

5 MD #2: Partner Drills with Down-Up [A ball and partner drill]

1. Consecutive Passing drill: Pass with their partner with full down up movement. Around 10 reps would be good to begin with.
2. Regular Partner passing: Pass back and forth with a partner in "Go" posture and with "Full Down-up" movement (15 repetitions minimum).
3. Back pass drill: Pass to themselves with full down-up movement and then turn around (backwards) to pass the ball to their partner with full down-up back passing.
4. Regular partner passing: Finish the sequence with regular partner down-up passing (10-15 repetitions).

Chapter 7: 5 Minute Drills **215**

VERY IMPORTANT NOTE

All of the drills you will see in the next section are "CONTROLLED drills." This means that the balls served and tossed are all controlled. Coaches or players who are running the drills must serve or toss with certain qualities, such as height, velocity and direction. The serving and tossing have to be in control or the players will never get the right feeling and timing for the skill being taught.

5 MD #3: Down-Up Passing Drill [With coaches tossing or serving]

The Tanden Passing Band™ forces passers to keep their arms close to their body and helps them to focus on Tanden passing instead of swinging their arms.

1. Down-up passing 1: Down-up passing from the "Go" position with coaches tossing. Lower the *platform down only as the knees bend. Then extend knees without swinging the platform (Lift the ball with the legs instead of the arms).* Hands should start from "Go" and then drop down to the Tanden area when standing up (20+ reps each player).

Cynthia Barboza, USA

2. Down-up passing 2: Do the same as above with coaches serving.
3. Side-to-side Down-up passing: Coach or player serves a relatively loopy ball to the passer going side-to-side to begin with, in order to let them feel the down-up movement. If the serve is too flat, the players won't be able

216 Inside Out of Passing

to feel the down-up movement. Players should move side-to-side with shuffle steps in the "Go" position and work on down-up passing. Do 10 or more repetitions on each side.

4. Down-up passing with movement 2: Pass the ball with forward and drop step movement in the "Go" position and work on down-up passing. Do more than 20 reps each player. Start the player on the 3 meter line. The coach or player serves a relatively loopy ball over the passer's head and then serves or tosses a short ball in front of the passer so they must move to the ball and then down-up pass to the target.

5 MD #4: Touch the Floor Down-Up Drill [With coaches tossing]

1. Touch the floor drill: Player passes the ball after touching the floor with down-up movement. Make sure that the passer touches the floor just before they pass to force the "UP" part of the down-up motion.

Tara Cross-Battle, USA

2. Both knees drop drill: Player waits for the ball on the floor on both knees in

"Go" position. Pass the ball with knee drop posture and then get up.

Ogonna Nnamani, USA

5 MD #5: Down-Up Passing Timing Control Drill
[With coaches serving]

1. 1-2-3 passing: 1-2-3 Serve Receive passing with coaches serving. The serve should be medium height and medium velocity. Passers should focus on the server. The serve is hit on 1. Down movement while bringing the platform down at 2 and contact or up movement at 3. Coaches and/or players should call 1-2-3. Do the drill for a couple of minutes until the passers pick-up the timing.

2. 2-3 passing: 2-3 Serve Receive passing with coaches serving. The serve should be flat and with high velocity. The coach can also serve off of a box for faster tempo serves. The passer should focus on the server for 1. When the serve is hit, it's already 2, and contact of the ball is on 3. Coaches and/or players should call 2-3. Do the drill for a couple minutes until the passers pick-up the quicker timing.

5 MD #6: Development of foot work to get behind the ball Drill #1

[With coaches tossing]

1. <u>Corner step drill or Circle Passing (pg. 88):</u> Players will shuffle along the outside corners on the court. Start in the corner and shuffle to the right or left along the lines following the coach's movement. Without a ball, players should focus on always lining up directly in front of the coach. Do this repetition 6 times.

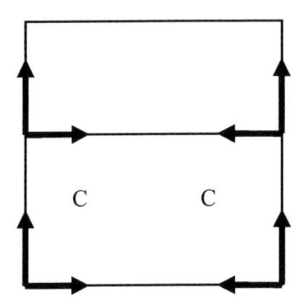

Diagram 4 : Corner Step Drill

2. <u>Corner step drill with coaches tossing:</u> Continue this drill using the corners of the court but with a coach tossing. Players should follow the coach's movements while staying on the lines and shuffle pass back to the coach.

Tara Cross-Battle, USA

5 MD #7: Development of footwork to get behind the ball Drill #2

[With coaches tossing]

1. Between legs drill with rolled ball: Coach rolls the ball. The player moves and tries to let the ball roll between their legs while maintaining "Go" posture. Shuffle steps should be used when moving. Do this drill 5 -7 times for each player.

2. Between legs drill with bounced ball 1: A coach tosses a high ball in front of the player or to their right or left. The player tries to let the ball bounce between their legs with shuffle steps (see Diagram 5).

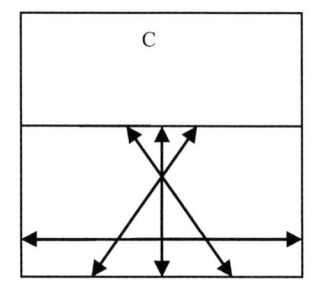

Diagram 5: Bounce ball between legs drill 1 & 2

3. Between legs drill with bounced ball 2: Do the above drill with forward and back movement. Shuffle forward and shuffle back steps should be used to get in position to let the ball bounce in between the passers legs.

5 MD #8: Development of footwork to get behind the ball Drill #3

220 Inside Out of Passing

(*Back-up passing drill*) [With coaches/player serving]

1. Back up passing drill: Player starts from the 3 meter line. The coach or player serves a loopy ball over the passer's head. Upon contact the passer backs up to get behind the ball and pass the ball, finishing forward towards the target.

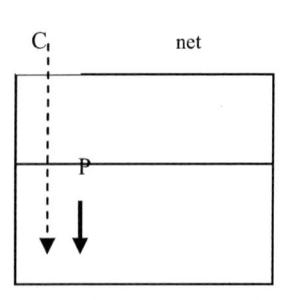

Diagram 6: Development of footwork to get behind the ball.

2. Diagonal back-up passing: The passer starts from the middle of the court. A coach or player serves diagonally and over the passer in the direction of the corner of the court. The passer should back up diagonally to get behind the ball and finish forward passing the ball the target (Diagram 7).

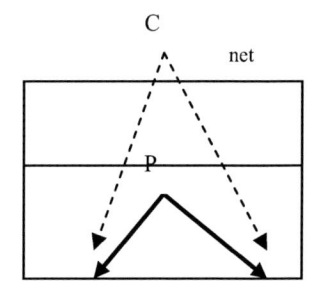

Diagram 7: Diagonal back-up passing

5 MD #9: Solid contact and compact platform movement Drill
[Individual drill or partner drill]

1. One hand wall pass: The passer should stand about 3 feet away from the wall. Pass the ball to the wall consecutively with a strong foundation with only one arm. This drill requires quick and very compact body movements. Try to do this at least 10 times in a row with each hand two times.

Chapter 7: 5 Minute Drills **221**

Tara Cross-Battle, USA

2. <u>Two hand wall pass:</u> The passer should stand about 3 feet away from the wall. Pass the ball to the wall consecutively with a strong foundation and a two hand platform. This drill requires quick and a very compact platform movement. Try to do this at least two sets of 10 to 20 passes in a row.

Tara Cross-Battle, USA

3. <u>One hand pass to self:</u> Passers should pass the ball to themselves consecutively low and fast with quick down-up movement of the lower body with only one hand. Try to do this at least 10 times in a row.

4. <u>Two hand pass to yourself with fast tempo</u>: Passers should pass the ball to themselves low and fast consecutively with quick down-up movement of the lower body. Try to do this at least 10 times in a row.

NOTE: The passers must focus on lifting the ball with their legs and allowing only minimal arm swing.

Tara Cross-Battle, USA

5 MD #10: Punch Technique Drill [With coaches tossing and serving]

1. Go-Punch-Go with coaches tossing: Passers should start in the "Go" position, punch pass on contact and then return to the "Go" position after the ball is passed. *Coaches must make sure that the passer bends their ankles and knees as they punch pass the ball.* Do this drill with 15 or more repetitions. The target should be 10 feet away from the passer in the beginning to force the passer to control the ball using the punch technique.

2. Go-Punch-Go with coaches serving medium speed: The same as above with coaches serving. Start with the target 10 feet away and progress the target back towards the net as the technique and control improve.

3. Go-Punch-Go with movement from coach's toss: Coaches move players from left to right with passers in "Go" posture. The passers should punch pass and then return to "Go" posture after the ball is passed. Do this drill more than 7 times on each side. Start with the target 10 feet away.

4. Go-Punch-Go with movement from coach's serve: Coaches move players from left to right with passers in "Go" posture. The passers should punch pass and then return to "Go" posture after the ball is passed. Do this drill more than 7 times on each side. Start with the target 10 feet away.

Coaches should have control to serve to the passer within one shuffle distance from the passer.

5 MD #11: Passing the flat float serve with high velocity Drill
[With coaches serving high velocity]

1. Ground serve passing drill: Coach serving on the ground about 40 feet from the passer. The serve should be a flat float serve with high velocity. Continue to do this drill for about 10 passes.
2. Consecutive passing drill 1: Initiate the drill the same as the ground serve passing drill, except that each player passes 5 to 6 balls in a row with a fast tempo. Coaches must serve balls one after another in quick succession. This drill is important because it forces automatic platform adjustments without time to think or over-analyze.
3. Box passing drill: Coach on a box at the end line serving players a flat float serve with high velocity. 10 repetitions at a time should be sufficient for this drill.
4. Consecutive passing drill 2: Initiate the drill like the box passing drill, except the passer must pass 5 to 6 balls in a row with a fast tempo. Coaches must serve one ball after another in quick succession. This drill is important because it forces automatic platform adjustments without time to think or over analyze.

5 MD #12: Adjustment Drill (angle and distance)

[With players/coaches serving]

1. Line Cross drill (Diagram 8) : Two players are on the court and pass the ball 6 times in a row. Coaches serve cross-court and down the line alternating at the same time. This drill forces the passer to see the other server in order to be ready for an immediate serve one after another.

2. Short Long drill (Diagram 9): One coach or player serves from about ten feet from the end line and the other one serves from the end line. The coaches alternate serves. Two players are on the court and pass 6 balls in a row. The passer must adjust their timing for a short serve and long serve and pass one after another.

3. Total adjustment drill (Diagram 10): One coach or player serves from the far diagonal corner to the diagonal passer and the other server stands at the end line directly in front of the passer. Servers alternate 6 passes in a row.

**For Advanced Players, the serve can be both a short serve and a long serve.

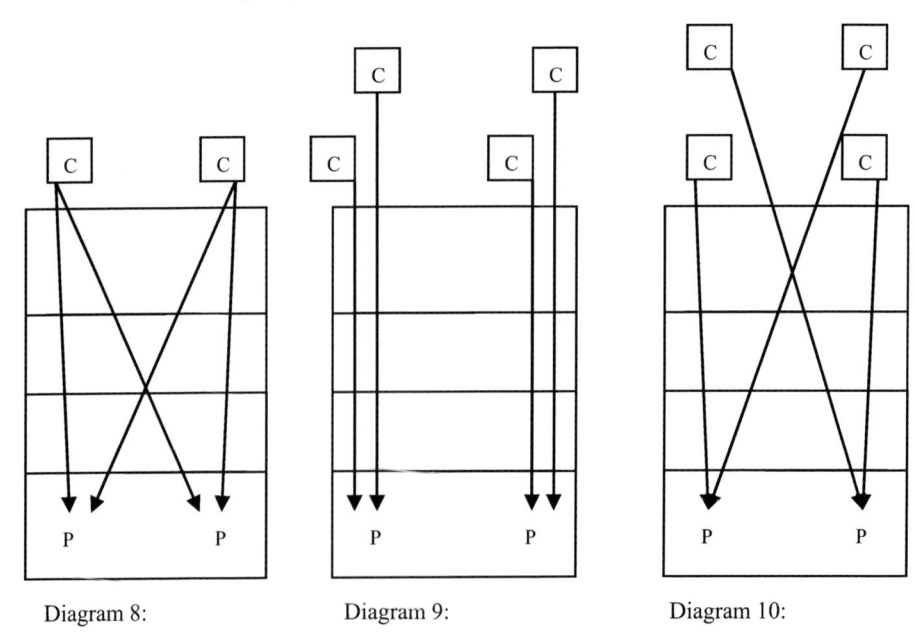

Diagram 8:
Line Cross Drill

Diagram 9:
Short- Deep Drill

Diagram 10:
Total Adjustment Drill

5 MD #13: Group Passing Drill (Learning the basic serve receive path of the passers) [With coaches/player serving]

1. Position 5 (P5) to middle (Diagram 11): A coach stands by the net and tosses a ball between the passers. The right side passer should cut off the ball and move in front of the left side player. The left side passer should go behind the right side passer once the ball is tossed. Do this drill about 10 times in order for the passers to get used to this movement. Then have the coaches or players serve from the end line in between the passers. The two passers should automatically move the path in order for the pathway of the passers to be defined accurately. The serve should be as accurate as possible.

2. Position 1 (P1) to middle (Diagram 12): A coach stands by the net and tosses a ball between the players. The left side passer should cut off the ball and move in front of the right side passer. The right side passer should go behind the left side passer once the ball is tossed. Do this drill about 10 times in order for the passers to get used to the movement. Then have the coach or player serve from the end line in between the passers. The two passers should automatically move the path in order for the pathway of the passers to be defined accurately.

3. Both directions (Diagram 13): Two coaches stand in different spots along the net and alternate tossing balls between passers. As C@P5, tosses the ball, two passers move the way I described the path in Diagram 11. As C@P1 tosses the ball, two passers move the way I described the path in Diagram 12. Repeat this drill for 6 passes.

226 Inside Out of Passing

Diagram 11:
Position 5 to middle

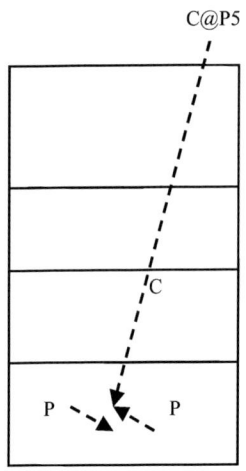

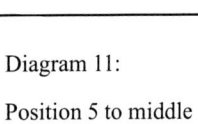

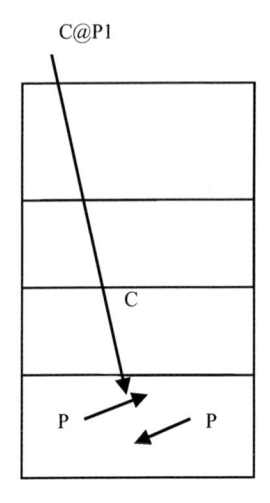

Diagram 12:
Position 1 to middle

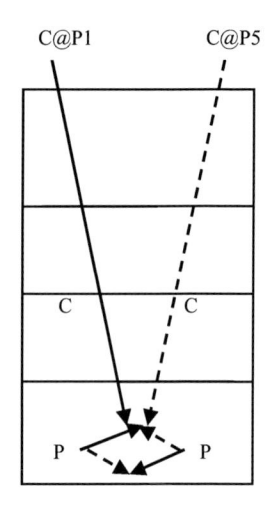

Diagram 13:
Both directions

5 MD #14: Key Oriented Drill [With coaches/player serving]

1. <u>Technique point drill:</u> In any kind of live passing drill, passers can score if they use a certain technique while performing the skill. A coach should evaluate whether or not they used a certain technique (such as down-up or punch pass). Do this type of point scoring drill for 5 minutes to see how many points a player can get.

5 MD #15: Concentration Drill [With Coaches/Player Serving]

1. <u>In a row drill:</u> A player stays in and passes the ball until 2 to 3 balls are passed perfectly in a row. This number would be increased depending upon the passers skill level.
2. <u>In a row drill with group:</u> Use this same drill with a group or team and increase the number of perfect passes the group must get in a row to finish.

The 5 minute drills I have covered are basic drills to develop the fundamentals of passing. These drills give you a very good idea of how to implement the 8 KEYS you have seen in this book.

APPENDIX

1) Goals for Passing

A Statistical Point of View

2) Linear Passing

GOALS FOR PASSING AS A TEAM

From a Statistical Point of View

The table below shows a comparison of the win and loss statistics of USA's execution in 1999.

Per Game		Attp	PP	PP%	E	E%	Avg
Win	Mean	10.7	7	61	0.70	3.90	2.40
	SD	53	1	13.9	0.58	3.33	0.04
Loss	Mean	22	12	56.6	1.5	7.79	2.26
	SD	2.97	3.22	9.6	1.38	5.65	0.26

These variables are per GAME

Attp: Total attempts per game

pp: number of perfect passes

pp%: number of perfect passes divided by the number of attempts* 100

E: number of reception errors per game

E%: number of reception errors divided by the number of attempts*100

Avg: average of evaluation by 4 points scale (0-3)

From the above results, the numbers in grey boxes would be the statistical goals for Team USA's passing. This has been USA's GOAL of Passing to win a game since 2000. Perfect passing percentage should be more than 61%. We are allowed to get aced less than one time per game. The reception error percentage should be less than 3.9% and our passing average should be more than 2.4.

We did not accomplish these goals for passing at the 2002 World Championships. Here are the averages for the games played in this competition.

<u>pp%:57%, E:1.1 , E%:5%, Avg:2.19</u>

Team USA is still inconsistent with passing and must improve in order to win the 2004 Olympics (December, 2002).

CHINA

PP%	E	E%	Avg
58.0	1.0	5.5	NA

RUSSIA

PP%	E	E%	Avg
54.8	0.7	4.0	NA

BRAZIL

PP%	E	E%	Avg
55.5	0.9	4.9	NA

LINEAR PASSING

Linear Passing is the Only Safe Pass in Volleyball

Coaching Volleyball. July/Aug 2002. Vol. 19. No4, pg 10.

In order to understand the essence of passing, which is the most important skill in volleyball, I must first define an area of the body that we can focus on. Unlike common belief indicating that a forearm pass is performed by the arms, it is the mid-section of the body that influences the absorption and re-direction of the ball. This area is near the center of gravity and is called TANDEN. The concept is that power in many sports originates from the Tanden area. One's power of punch or arm swing is initiated from the Tanden. This concept is also applied to the baseball throw, baseball batting, a receivers catching technique in football and many instances in karate, boxing and kendo. Just an arm swing lacks the desired power to perform adequately. The power comes from the Tanden with the arms correlating. In fact, there should be a connection between the arms and the Tanden. Non-linear passing disrupts this connection.

In Tanden passing, the passer should absorb the velocity of the ball close to the body (Tanden). If one receives the ball outside the frame of the body, the passer cannot absorb the speed and control the ball in correlation with Tanden. For controlling a pass, a player needs timing, a good platform and good contact. Good contact should transmit power from the Tanden. Whenever a passer's arms exert power outside the frame of the body, the connection with Tanden is minimized, therefore the power to exert and control is compromised.

When a contact point is supported by the body directly behind it, the power of the body supports the action. If the contact point is outside the body, the required power cannot be supported adequately. When one wants to push a heavy load, the pusher's hands are placed in front of their midline. If the pusher's hands exert force from outside the mid-line, it will be an insufficient force.

Passing Linear means passing between one's knees. In this position the passer can have efficient power contacting the ball. In order to reduce the chances of a shank (bad miss), the player must stabilize the upper body and reduce arm-swing. Passing a slow moving ball, a player can swing their arms or receive a ball outside of their body frame with some degree of success. But it is extremely difficult to have success passing or digging a hard driven ball outside one's body frame.

Passing Linear with a tight-to-the-body forearm platform is a technique that can reduce arm swing because there is no room for axis rotation. Passing success is directly related to connecting the line of rebound to the Tanden.

ABOUT THE AUTHOR

TOSHI YOSHIDA
Head Coach, USA Women's National Volleyball Team

Toshi Yoshida was hired by USA Volleyball in 2001 as the head coach of the USA Women's National Volleyball Team. From 2001-2004, Yoshida has led the team to a third place finish at the 2003 World Cup which qualified the USA team for a spot in the 2004 Olympic Games in Athens, Greece. He also led the team to a second place finish at the 2002 World Championships and a No. 3 world ranking, as well as a gold medal performance at the 2001 World Grand Prix.

Yoshida was named the head coach of the USA Women's National Volleyball Team in November 2000 after replacing Mick Haley who returned to the collegiate ranks as the head coach of the University of Southern California. Yoshida served as the assistant coach of the USA women's team from 1979-83 and then again from 1998-2000. With Yoshida's involvement with the team, the team progressed from a No.10 world ranking to finishing 4th at the 2000 Olympic Games in Sydney, Australia.

Yoshida brings a wealth of volleyball experience, both as a player and as a coach. Yoshida was hired as the trainer for the Hitachi Club Team in 1978 of which many of those players formed the 1976 Olympic Gold Medal Team. He then joined the USA Women's National Volleyball Team in September 1979 as an assistant coach, helping the team place third in the 1982 World Championships and fourth in the 1981 World Cup. Yoshida returned to Japan in 1983 to lead the Hitachi LTD Club to the 16th Japanese League title in 1982-83. From 1983-97, Yoshida was the head volleyball coach and associate professor at Tokyo Gukugei University. Yoshida spent one year as the head coach of the Tierp Volleyball Club of Sweden before rejoining the USA women's national team staff in 1998. Yoshida and his wife, Shoko, are the parents of a 21-year-old daughter, Yoko.

ABOUT THE EDITORS

Advanced Sports Training was developed to make innovative, current volleyball techniques available to all athletes. We believe that players advancing their volleyball knowledge and skills through our active, dynamic training sessions increase their self-confidence and self-esteem. **Advanced Sports Training** strives to introduce and advance volleyball skills using exciting and creative methods that encourage learning and understanding. We believe that advancing athletes in a team atmosphere helps them to create a more successful future in sports and life.

To keep us ahead of the rest we have partnered with **Toshi Yoshida** and members of his staff and team to help bring youth volleyball to the next level. Players camps and Coaches clinics are being scheduled around the nation using Coach Yoshida's elite training techniques and systems.

Under the instruction of Coach Yoshida, **Advanced Sports Training** plans to bring world-class volleyball instruction into youth programs across the nation, upon your request. For more information, please contact:

Advanced Sports Training
PO Box 2215
Costa Mesa, CA 92628
805-402-1417 (office)
866-851-3873 (fax)
www.advancedsports.org